Paul the Apostle

Photography by Erich Lessing

Translated by Timothy J. Hallett

PAUL THE APOSTLE

Edward Schillebeeckx

CROSSROAD · NEW YORK

Documentation in the Index of Illustrations by Dr. Alfred Bernhard-Walcher, of the Kunsthistorisches Museum, Antikensammlung, Vienna.

1983
The Crossroad Publishing Company
575 Lexington Avenue, New York, N. Y. 10022

Originally published under the title *Paulus—Der Völkerapostel*
© Verlag Herder Freiburg im Breisgau 1982

English translation copyright © 1983 by The Crossroad Publishing Company

Printed in West Germany

Library of Congress Cataloging in Publication Data
Schillebeeckx, Edward, 1914–
    Paul the Apostle.
    Translation of Paulus der Völkerapostel.
    Includes index.
    1. Paul, the Apostle, Saint. 2. Christian saints—Turkey—Tarsus—Biography. 3. Tarsus (Turkey)—Biography. 4. Mediterranean Region—Description and travel—Views. I. Title.
BS2506.S2713 1983   225.9'24 [B]   82-22078
ISBN 0-8245-0574-3

CONTENTS

WHAT DO WE KNOW ABOUT PAUL?

Our information about Paul comes from two sources: the Acts of the Apostles, written by Luke, the Greek physician who intermittently accompanied Paul on his journeys; and the letters written by Paul—and also, as we shall see, by followers of Paul—to the congregations which he had founded. These two sources provide a lively account of many incidents in the life of the "Apostle of the Gentiles." Yet they constitute not so much an actual biography of Paul as a spiritual history of that early Christianity in which Paul played an essential role.

The search for exact dates on which to base the biographical framework of Paul's life yields only such figures as scholarship can coax from the sources. The year A. D. 10 has been reckoned as the approximate date of Paul's birth. Paul's father was a freeman of Tarsus in Asia Minor and possessed a Roman citizenship which was inherited by his son. As a young man, Paul traveled from his home in Tarsus to Jerusalem in order to study the Torah under the renowned Rabbi Gamaliel. He may have arrived in Jerusalem in about A. D. 30; certainly it was only after the death of Jesus, for otherwise Paul would have mentioned in one of his letters that he had seen Jesus in person. Paul, whose family was of the tribe of Benjamin, had been raised in a strict Pharisaic environment. This fundamental attitude explains his hatred of the nascent Christian movement, a hostility especially evident in the stoning of Stephen. That event may have taken place in about A. D. 35, and Paul probably participated as an official observer.

Paul's "conversion" on the road to Damascus, where he intended to implement a similar persecution of Christians, most likely occurred that same year, in 35. Paul the Christian, now himself the object of persecution, fled from Damascus to "Arabia." Not until three years later, in about A. D. 38, did he go to Jerusalem, where he met Peter and the other apostles. After only fifteen days he traveled on to his home in Tarsus.

We may assume that Paul proclaimed his message of Christ in his homeland, Cilicia. Otherwise it would hardly have occurred to Barnabas, who was a leader of the flourishing Christian community at Antioch on the Orontes, to bring Paul the Christian zealot to Antioch in about the year 43 and later, in 44, to take him along to Jerusalem. There they delivered the collection from the community at Antioch to the Christian community of Jerusalem, which was suffering persecution. The apostle James had only recently been executed by King Herod Agrippa.

One year later, in 45, Barnabas took Paul with him on a missionary journey which led via Cyprus to Asia Minor. This missionary journey lasted almost five years. During its course, leadership was gradually, imperceptibly assumed by Paul. The most important stations on the way were at Perga, Pisidian Antioch, Iconium, Lystra, and Derbe.

Immediately upon their return the two missionaries decided to go from Antioch to Jerusalem in order to report to the apostles on their experiences in the mission to the Gentiles. The Apostolic Council in Jerusalem took place around A.D. 50. It was there that Paul obtained from the Jewish-Christian apostles an endorsement of his mission to the Gentiles.

Inspired by this official endorsement, Paul embarked the same year on his second missionary journey. This took him via Asia Minor to Macedonia, then to Athens, where he experienced failure, and on to Corinth. Paul remained in Corinth for almost two years. While there he wrote his first letter to the Thessalonians. At last, in 53, he sailed via Miletus to Caesarea, and journeyed via Jerusalem to Antioch.

After a brief sojourn, the tireless Apostle set out on his third missionary journey. This journey, after visits to the congregations in Asia Minor, led to Ephesus, where Paul remained for two years. A disturbance caused by the pagan silversmiths there resulted in Paul's expulsion from the city. After revisiting the congregations in Macedonia and Greece, he returned to ship, stopping at Miletus. While there he summoned the elders of the congregations of Ephesus and Asia Minor for a monitory farewell address. It was Paul's intention now to travel from Jerusalem via Rome to Spain.

When Paul arrived in Jerusalem in A.D. 58, zealous Jews incited a riot against him. He was arrested by the Romans and remanded to the custody of the Procurator Felix in Caesarea. Paul insisted on his right as a Roman citizen to be tried before an imperial court. He was subsequently sent to Rome.

The ship with the prisoner Paul sailed from Caesarea in autumn of the year 60. A shipwreck, followed by severe storms, necessitated wintering on Malta. It was not until 61 that Paul set foot on Italian soil.

In Rome, Paul was kept under loose arrest for two years. We do not know whether his case was ever heard before a court. We are equally ignorant of the possibility of any further journeyings by the Apostle. The martyrdom of Paul is reported only by second-century sources. As a Roman citizen, he may have been beheaded, perhaps in A.D. 67.

Travel 2000 Years Ago

The Acts of the Apostles records Paul's journeys, but for all practical purposes it does little more than list the locations which the Apostle visited. At the beginning of the third missionary journey, Luke simply states: "... he departed and went from place to place through the region of Galatia and Phrygia ..." (Acts 18:23). Yet that meager summary conceals a physical feat which is scarcely conceivable to persons of the twentieth century. We are accustomed to traveling by automobile, train, and airplane, and our walking tours consist primarily of short strolls on Sunday afternoons. Erich Lessing, who retraced the footsteps of the Apostle in order to take the photographs for this volume, needed three rental cars to complete his journeys in Asia Minor. They fell victim to the potholes in the terrible roads of the Cilician highlands. Mr. Lessing was more than happy when his exhausting travels were at an end. If a twentieth-century traveler experiences hardship in the course of a motor trip in the regions of the Pauline mission, then the Lukan account is indeed an understatement.

Let us trace the course of Paul's third journey: He left Antioch on the Orontes, walking northwards. With the temperature at thirty degrees Celsius he may have made twenty-five kilometers a day. But this daily pace must soon have slackened, for the road led uphill. Therefore it would have taken Paul about ten days to reach the gateway to Cilicia, a narrow pass which permits penetration of the Taurus Mountains. The altitude of the pass is 1000 meters; the peaks of the mountains range as high as 3000 meters. From that point Paul had 1000 kilometers to go before reaching the port of Troas, where he could board ship for Macedonia. If some contemporary record-seeker were to attempt a 1200 kilometer trek across the sun-baked plateau of Asia Minor, his achievement would be reported in every newspaper. Yet the conditions for Paul and his companions were incomparably more difficult than for a modern hiker. By day, they would have sustained themselves with a handful of dates and an occasional sip of water. In the evening they might have eaten a thin gruel or a piece of flatbread and, if lucky, a fish from one of the streams or a piece of cheese from a shepherd whose hut could also provide shelter for the night.

When Paul came upon a place which he had already visited, where there were friends and a congregation, the meal would have been somewhat better. Perhaps a roast goat would be prepared in welcome, and there would be a drink of wine. But the members of the Christian communities in the highlands were by and large as poor as Paul himself. The simple lifestyle of these first Christians is almost beyond our imagination. Paul himself took pride in never burdening his congregations, a fact he emphasizes in 1 Thessalonians: "We worked night and day, that we might not burden any of you. ..." And in 2 Thessalonians he writes: "We were not idle when we were with you, we did not eat anyone's bread without paying, but with toil and labor we worked night and day, that we might not burden any of you."

How Did Paul Support Himself?

We know that Paul had learned the trade of tentmaking, although—or precisely because—he had originally intended to become a rabbi. For by Jewish tradition, rabbis and scribes were expected to be able to earn their own living. Thus, Paul operated as an itinerant tradesman, hiring himself out as a tentmaker in a master's shop in those places where he lingered for a time. His activity as a missionary and preacher of the gospel would have been confined to the Sabbath. His wages would have been barely sufficient for frugal living, since he had to put aside some savings to finance his winter travels. His thank-you letter to the Philippians gives us some sense of how poorly the apostle lived while on his journeys: "... even in Thessalonica you sent me help once and again .... I have received full payment, and more; I am filled, having received ... the gifts you sent ...." The expression "I am filled" bears witness to the frugality of the indefatigable "servant of Jesus Christ." For fullness is not abundance and luxury; it simply means that for a while Paul need not work all day for his livelihood and therefore can devote all his time to preaching.

Our amazement increases when we remember that this tireless traveler was not in good health. Twice in his letters we find reference to his illness. In 2 Corinthians Paul writes: "And to keep me from being too elated ... a thorn was given me in the flesh .... Three times I besought the Lord about this, that it should leave me; but he said to me, 'My grace is sufficient for you, for my power is made perfect in weakness.'" And in the letter to the Galatians Paul states: "You know it was because of a bodily ailment that I preached the gospel to you at first." We know nothing of the illness which the Apostle periphrastically calls his "thorn in the flesh." We know only that he shrugged off his suffering—and it must have been chronic—and proclaimed his gospel despite it. One is struck by the fact that pictures of Paul invariably portray him as thin-faced, often with sunken cheeks. When one considers the privations which Paul had to endure on his travels—thousands of kilometers by foot, meager nourishment—one might arrive at the diagnosis that Paul suffered a chronic stomach ailment resulting from poor nutrition and continuous stress.

Now I Speak

So far we have encountered a Paul who selflessly and humbly fulfilled the commission entrusted to him by his Lord. We have seen a man who withdrew behind his work, made no fuss about the hardships of his travels, and continued his preaching despite his illness. Only once— in 2 Corinthians 11—does he drop his reserve in a passage which substantially increases our knowledge of Paul as a person. The passage is motivated by the Apostle's concern that his congregation was being seduced by certain self-proclaimed "superlative apostles" or "superapostles," and might be deflected from the true gospel as he himself had preached it. Paul thunders: "such men are false apostles, deceitful workmen, disguising themselves as apostles of Christ." Because these false missionaries have openly boasted about their deeds and merits, Paul asserts his right to do the same. He is aware that in doing so he is not speaking "with the Lord's authority." Nonetheless he continues: "But whatever anyone dares to boast of ... I also dare to boast of that .... Are they servants of Christ? I am a better one—I am talking like a madman— with far greater labors, far more imprisonments, with countless beatings, and often near death. Five times I have received at the hands of the Jews the forty lashes less one. Three times I have been beaten with rods; once I was stoned. Three times I have been shipwrecked; a night and a day I have been adrift at sea; on frequent journeys, in danger from rivers, danger from robbers, danger from my own people, danger from Gentiles, danger in the city, danger in the wilderness, danger at sea, danger from false brethren; in toil and hardship, through many a sleepless night, in hunger and thrist, often without food, in cold and exposure. And, apart from other things, there is the daily pressure upon me of my anxiety for all the churches."

In righteous indignation Paul vented his feelings and presented the wavering Corinthians with a list of his sufferings and privations. No doubt many of the members of his congregation were shocked by this news, for they had been ignorant of these incidents. And they could immediately grasp—far better than any modern reader—the degree of these sufferings. Paul had borne the punishments commonly meted out to criminals, and such punishments were administered in public. Thus they knew that the "forty stripes save one" which Paul had endured five times meant that in five instances he had been beaten just short of death. The "less one" meant that by the thirty-ninth blow the point had been reached where any additional blow might result in the death of the offender. Ancient justice was experienced in such things.

Three times he had been scourged. The Corinthians also knew that the strokes of the scourge ripped the skin in shreds from the body. It was weeks before the person thus punished could recover—if indeed he survived and did not die of blood poisoning or gangrene.

As for stoning, that meant death in the slowest, most horrible fashion. Anyone who survived a stoning could indeed speak of a miracle. Paul was fortunate enough to escape his stoning in Lystra because it was assumed that he was dead.

A Shipwreck Expert

"Three times I have been shipwrecked; a night and a day I have been adrift at sea." Behind this statement too lies an unimaginable degree of hardship. To keep one's head above water for twenty-four hours after shipwreck is a feat which can be accomplished only by a person of great courage and endurance.

Paul repeatedly crossed the Aegean Sea in the course of his travels to Greece and back to Asia Minor and Syria. Anyone who knows how quickly a storm can brew in the Aegean will realize that a boat voyage in antiquity was an adventure. The ships on which the Apostle traveled were little cargo sailers, two-masters at most, and their clumsy sails offered small scope for maneuvering in sudden squalls. Beyond that, Paul must have traveled primarily on old ships, real "tubs" which had long outlived any seaworthiness. Still, passage on such ships was cheap, and that was an important point. These ships had no cabins, at any rate not for have-nots like Paul and his companions. They went as deck passengers and had to crouch close to the sides of the ship for protection against wind and waves. There, in the way of the seamen working the sails, they would be the recipients of frequent kicks and rough curses. And because sailors are generally quite superstitious, the missionary travelers, perhaps unawares, would have been in double jeopardy of their lives on stormy crossings. In the midst of the storm it could all too easily occur to the sailors: "Poseidon, god of the sea, is angry with us because there are men on board who do not believe in him. Perhaps the sea will calm if we throw these men overboard!"

If we read between the lines of Luke's account of the shipwreck off Malta, we can see that the sailors may have entertained such thoughts. To lighten the ship in the storm, part of the cargo was thrown overboard, then "the third day they cast out with their own hands the tackle of the ship." Undoubtedly the passengers would have been the next to go overboard. Paul must have sensed this—he was, after all, an experienced traveler. Just at the moment of greatest danger he calmed the sailors with a revelation: "This very night there stood by me an angel of the God to whom I belong and whom I worship, and he said, 'Do not be afraid, Paul; you must stand before Caesar; and lo, God has granted you all those who sail with you.'" Paul understood the superstitious sailors and knew that a divine revelation would give them confidence. He had saved the situation. And then, as an expert in shipwrecks, he virtually assumed command and finally saved the whole ship's company.

Paul the Man

We can approach the Apostle of the Gentiles from two directions. One perspective is that of the theologians who investigate Paul's religious message. Luke, the chronicler of the Acts of the Apostles was the first to take this course. His report is accurate if, as is believed, he almost literally quotes the great speeches and sermons of Paul. Yet, like Paul himself, he withholds almost everything which might shed light on Paul as a person. Hundreds of commentaries have been written on Paul's epistles. The question of authenticity is as much a subject of investigation as every theological statement. In 1515 and 1516 Martin Luther, as professor of theology at Wittenberg, delivered lectures on the epistles to the Romans and Galatians. Such lectures continue today.

The personality of Paul tends to get short shrift in these scholarly theological studies. Only a few scholars have sought to pose the question: What kind of man was Paul? Yet the sources, if read between the lines, offer much material which not only shows Paul as the great proclaimer who brought the message of Christ crucified to all the world but also reveals Paul as a man of flesh and blood. This introduction is intended to bring to life this Paul, this man so filled with courage, endurance, spirit, and humility.

It was this man Paul who first wholeheartedly undertook the "imitation of Christ." He had never met Jesus in person, but he was in many respects closer to Christ and assimilated his message better than many of the apostles personally called by Jesus. Paul's battle against the strictures of the Jewish "law" are proof of his superior understanding of the example Jesus had set for his disciples. Jesus, to the concealed horror of his disciples, had eaten with tax collectors; he had told them the parable of the Good Samaritan; he had viewed the question of Sabbath observance more liberally than the rigid Pharisees. Such indications were proof to Paul of the rightness of his own imitative action and the appropriateness of his mission to the Gentiles.

A beautiful example of Paul's unique understanding of Jesus' intention is found in 1 Corinthians. As his testament, so to speak, Jesus had given his disciples a new commandment: "That you love one another. By this all men will know that you are my disciples, if you have love for one another" (Jn. 13:34–35). Paul took this commandment of Jesus as his guiding principle. And this love, true love of neighbor, he preached to his congregations: "If I speak in the tongues of men and of angels, but have not love, I am a noisy gong or a clanging cymbal. And if I have prophetic powers, and understand all mysteries and all knowledge, and if I have all faith, so as to remove mountains, but have not love, I am nothing. If I give away all I have, and if I deliver my body to be burned, but have not love, I gain nothing.

"Love is patient and kind; love is not jealous or boastful; it is not arrogant or rude. Love does not insist on its own way; it is not irritable or resentful; it does not rejoice at wrong, but rejoices in the right. Love bears all things, believes all things, hopes all things, endures all things. Love never ends; as for prophecies, they will pass away; as for tongues, they will cease; as for knowledge, it will pass away ....

"So faith, hope, love abide, these three; but the greatest of these is love" (1 Cor. 13:1–8, 13).

In all the epistles of the Apostle of the Gentiles there is no passage which bears clearer witness to Paul's character as a person. These lines, so moving in their depth of insight, bring to life that man who could endure any suffering, any hardship in the service of Jesus Christ. He could do so because he was completely imbued with the new commandment of Christ.

This love of Christ and love of humankind impels the statement which most vividly recapitulates the whole enterprise of his mission and the whole chain of his sufferings: "We preach Christ crucified, a stumbling block to Jews and folly to Gentiles, but to those who are saved, both Jews and Greeks, Christ the power of God and the wisdom of God (1 Cor. 1:23–24)."

Had Paul not already borne the honored title of Apostle, history surely would have accorded him the sobriquet "the Great."

Paul and His World

This book represents a threefold effort to enliven for the modern reader the fascinating figure of the Apostle of the Gentiles. Edward Schillebeeckx casts light on the strategy of the missionary journeys and elucidates by means of the Apostle's letters the distinctiveness of Paul's proclamation of Christ. He demonstrates, especially through his interpretation of the deutero-Pauline epistles (letters written after Paul's death but nonetheless put forward under his name) how Paul's message changed in the course of development, how other aspects of his preaching came to the fore, and how the influence of his teaching was felt in later centuries.

Erich Lessing has retraced the travels of the Apostle. His photographs illustrate the sites of Paul's activity and provide examples of the depiction of Paul in early portraits and scenes. Accompanying the illustrations are key texts from the Acts of the Apostles, the Pauline letters, and the apocryphal Acts of Paul, which constitute the third avenue of our approach to Paul.

The aim of this book and its contributors is the same as that of Bishop Clement of Rome, the third successor of Peter, when he wrote to the Corinthians in about A. D. 93: "Let us set before our eyes the good apostles .... Paul showed how to win the prize of patient endurance: seven times he was in bonds, he was banished, he was stoned, he became a messenger (of the gospel) in both east and west, and earned well-merited fame for his faith; for he taught righteousness to the whole world, having traveled to the limits of the west; and when he had borne his witness before the rulers, he departed from the world an outstanding example of patient endurance."[*]

The figure of Paul, who proclaimed Christ and his message for over thirty years, has lost nothing of its topicality, even to the present day.

[*] 1 Clem. 5. 3, 5–7. Translated by Holly H. Graham in vol. 2 of *The Apostolic Fathers,* edited by Robert M. Grant. (New York: Thomas Nelson and Sons, 1965), pp. 25–26.

Edward Schillebeeckx

THE APOSTLE OF THE GENTILES AND HIS INFLUENCE

A certain one-sided picture of Paul's apostolic travels has taken hold in the minds of many Christians. This view, drawn in part from the book of Acts, takes the following general form: impelled by the expectation of Jesus' imminent return as Lord, Paul traveled feverishly, compulsively, almost randomly from city to city, preached in each place some rudimentary sermons, experienced a variety of attendant tribulations, then pressed ever onwards to other regions. The ultimate goal of this urgent, itinerant apostolate was to proceed via Asia Minor to Rome.

This facile account of events tallies neither with the verifiable historical facts nor with the Apostle's own understanding of his task.

The Pastoral Strategy of Paul's Missionary Journeys

The first missionary journey was launched from Antioch on the Orontes and proceeded via Cyprus to Cilicia in Asia Minor. Barnabas, not Paul, was formally invested with leadership, and in the course of the journey the gospel was preached in a number of relatively small cities (Paphos, Perga, Pisidian Antioch, Iconium, Lystra, and Derbe). This journey was something of an exception. Historical study has shown that when Paul himself was in charge, he proceeded according to a very careful plan. His pastoral objective was clear: in every instance he was determined to establish a *stable Christian community,* an effort which invariably required approximately two years on location. Furthermore, these congregations were established in carefully selected cities, namely the metropoles of the eastern and western provinces of the Roman Empire, the principal cities of the then-known "world." Above all, Paul chose cities which, because of their geographical, economic, and cultural-political position, could qualify as "world ports." These cities enjoyed a very important role as centers of attraction, and their influence extended over wide areas. Having formed a stable congregation in one of these cities, Paul could travel on, leaving behind an established Christian community which in turn could serve as a missionary center (to Paul, "church" always implies mission) for the evangelization of regional cities both near and far. The flourishing congregation at Antioch functioned as a vital missionary center and apparently served as a model in Paul's strategy. Paul and Barnabas had undertaken their first missionary journey by commission of the Christian community at Antioch.

Antioch on the Orontes had been founded as the capital of the Seleucid Empire. A review of the principal locales of the Pauline mission will reveal sites of comparable significance. *Philippi* was a highly important Roman colony in Greece, a point of contact between Greece (Macedonia) and the rest of the western world. Similarly, *Thessalonica* was the capital of the province of Macedonia; *Corinth* was the capital of the province of Achaia (middle and southern Greece). The latter was an industrial city with metal-working and ceramic establishments; it was also a city of great cultural activity, with chariot racing, music, and athletics. Indeed, in Paul's day Corinth was the preeminent Greek cultural city, pagan through and through. Corinth was also the banking center of the Graeco-Roman world.

Ephesus, while not the actual capital of the proconsulate of Asia (Perga was the official site), was nevertheless the residence of the Governor of Asia, and it enjoyed very lively relations with Corinth. Ephesus was at the time one of the greatest cities of the world. Besides being an important seaport, the city was world-famous for its Artemision, a temple of Artemis (the Greek name of the goddess) or Diana (her Roman name). This goddess was a Hellenistic reinterpretation of the age-old Asiatic *Magna Mater* or Great Mother, the divine symbol of fertility. The Temple of Diana was the grandest edifice of the entire Hellenistic period, one of the seven wonders of the ancient world. Construction was of marble throughout, and the roof rested on 127 Ionic columns. The temple made Ephesus an ancient Mecca, the goal of countless pilgrims drawn from every quarter of the world.

Finally, there was *Athens.* By Paul's time, the glory of the city had already faded; and while it remained the "city of philosophers," the Athens of the period was little more than a snobbish, half-dead city living on the memory of its monumental past. Perhaps Paul discerned no nascent potential for building a congregation in Athens; perhaps his attempt to do so was ill-starred. In the Acts of the Apostles, Luke provides a masterful account of the factors which militated against founding a congregation in that city (Acts 17:16–34). It would appear from Paul's later correspondence to the Corinthians (1 Cor. 1:18–25; 2:1–5) that he learned a lesson from his failure in Athens.

From this survey of sites it almost seems that Paul planned his missionary journeys with some ancient equivalent of Baedeker or the *Michelin Guide* at hand. What, then, moved Paul to bring the gospel to the remote, rough Galatians (Celts) of mainland Ancyra (modern Ankara)? This seems quite out of harmony with his missionary tactics. Yet he not only conducted a mission there; he also wrote a significant letter to these simple people, albeit without reference to any city. We learn from Acts 16:6–7 that it was apparently not his intention to Christianize the mainland. He evidently intended only to travel via Galatia and Phrygia to Bithynia, to the coast of the Black Sea and its many seaports. These port cities were important to his strategy.

These plans suggest that Paul's primary targets were seaports, not merely capital cities. For from seaports his message of the crucified and risen Christ could be carried worldwide, and in the form in which he himself had preached it. In his letter to the Galatians, Paul states the real reason for his seemingly "random" missionary activity on the mainland of Asia Minor: "You know it was because of a bodily ailment that I preached the gospel to you at first" (Gal. 4:13). As Paul was passing through Galatia, which lay across his travel route, he was forced by illness to halt for a time. While there, he made a virtue of necessity and preached the gospel.

It is established, then, that Paul did not travel aimlessly hither and thither, bringing the gospel to any city that happened to lie in his path. He intentionally limited his personal mission and activity to certain obvious, strategic locations, especially seaports, which served as focal points of the international intercourse of the time. Paul was by no means concerned only with the conversion of individuals; indeed, he seldom baptized anyone himself. His goal was *to build up the church*, for he knew that once he had established a viable congregation he would leave behind a new center of missionary activity. Thus, an entire region was evangelized by the congregation Paul had founded in Ephesus (1 Cor. 4:12–13). Paul himself writes from Ephesus to Corinth: "The churches of Asia send greetings" (1 Cor. 16:19). He also mentions Laodicea, Hierapolis, and Colossae, cities whose churches were founded by Epaphras (Col. 1:6–8; 4:12–13). Likewise, the address "to the church of God which is at Corinth, with all the saints who are in the whole of Achaia" (2 Cor. 1:1) indicates that the church in Corinth had founded a number of new congregations throughout Achaia. This pattern of missionary activity was also characteristic of the congregation at Thessalonica: "For not only has the word of the Lord sounded forth from you in Macedonia and Achaia, but your faith has gone forth everywhere . . ." (1 Thess. 1:8).

Paul's pastoral methodology involved the founding of churches in principal cities and the concurrent establishment of new centers of mission. This methodology must have required longer sojourns in the several cities than is indicated in the schematic account of the book of Acts. Paul did indeed believe that the Lord's return was near at hand. But he was not preoccupied with an irrational sense of eschatological urgency. On the contrary, he implemented a carefully considered plan to establish churches in cities from which the good news could be further spread abroad. In the epistle to the Romans, Paul writes: "From Jerusalem and as far round as Illyricum I preached the gospel of Christ" (Rom. 15:19b). By that time, he had conceived a plan to press on from Rome to Spain, for he apparently considered "his work" in the eastern portion of the empire to be complete, even though he had visited only the most important cities. Pauline Christianity was indeed an "urban" Christianity, not a rural religiosity.

Paul's missionary journeys were conducted according to a definite missionary code. He engaged in missionary activity only in areas in which Christian communities had not been previously established by Christians representing other, non-Pauline traditions. It was his ambition "to preach the gospel, not where Christ has already been named, lest I build on another man's foundation" (Rom. 15:20). In some of the cities in which Paul launched a mission, there were doubtless already some few Christians gathered as a house church; but there was not yet a real *community*. And in his missionary travels, Paul was engaged in laying the foundations of strong Christian communities.

15

Against this background, we may compare the book of Acts with the authentic Pauline epistles and attempt to reconcile the accounts in Acts with Pauls's own concept of church formation. We shall find that, in broad outline, there is substantial agreement between the Lukan reports of the two or three so-called missionary journeys and Paul's personal recollections of the same. But we shall also see that the Acts of the Apostles betrays many gaps in information and provides a heavily schematized account, especially in relation to periods of time. Moreover, the interpretation of the journeys is dominated by a distinctively Lukan view of salvation history and of the development of the primitive church. Luke records a history which is directed westward, toward Rome.

Paul in the Acts of the Apostles

The Acts of the Apostles presents Paul's journeys as if, in all his travels, he looked toward Rome as the ultimate goal, the climax of his worldwide apostolic activity. Nothing could be farther from the truth. In the first place, to target Rome as a goal would have been a contradiction of Paul's own missionary code, for Rome already had a flourishing Christian community, with a membership composed perhaps predominantly, but not exclusively, of Jewish Christians. At the close of his pastoral career in Asia and Greece, prior to his final journey to Jerusalem, Paul wrote a letter from Corinth to the Christian community at Rome, announcing a forthcoming visit. The letter was written solely to advise the brethren there of his intention to conduct a mission in Spain and to indicate his plan to pass through Rome *en route.* To Paul, the anticipated sojourn in Rome was to be a stop along the way; his journey was not being undertaken for the purpose of preaching the gospel in that city: "... Now, since I no longer have any room for work in these regions, and since I have longed for many years to come to you, *I hope to see you in passing as I go to Spain,* and to be sped on my journey there by you, *once I have enjoyed your company for a little"* (Rom. 15:23–24). Indeed, Paul states a second time his intention merely to pause in Rome along the way: "When I have completed this [delivery of the collection of the churches of Macedonia and Achaia to Jerusalem] and have delivered to them what has been raised, I shall go on *by way of you* to Spain" (Rom. 15:28).

It is clear, then, that Rome was not the goal of this apostolic journey. Paul had in mind instead a sort of "apostolic holiday," a vacation in a sister congregation while on the way to his real destination. Paul's actual goal was Spain, the extreme western limit of the then-known world. Upon arrival in Jerusalem, however, Paul became entangled in difficulties which led first to his arrest (Acts 21:27–37) and ultimately to his appeal to the Emperor in Rome (Acts 25:11–12). The result was a trip to Rome under circumstances entirely at variance with Paul's plans. It was an eventful voyage: a shipwreck off Malta made it necessary to winter on the island. On arrival in Rome, Paul was placed under close house arrest. The conditions of arrest were later relaxed, and he remained in Rome for a period of two years (Acts 27–28). Beyond that, we know very little, except that he was eventually beheaded outside the city walls. We do not know whether the execution was official or a lynching; Paul may have been the victim of some kind of pogrom. In either case, there is among historians a growing consensus that Paul died some years prior to the accession of Nero, and not during the latter's reign. Any suggestion that Paul did in fact eventually undertake a journey to Spain is either pure conjecture or pious fantasy, with no historical basis. Paul proposes, God disposes.

The accounts of Paul's travels in the Acts of the Apostles are colored by Luke's own interpretation of salvation history. Nevertheless, Acts clearly recognizes that the establishment of the Christian community at Ephesus represented to Paul the completion of his mission in the eastern half of the Roman Empire (Acts 16:6–10; Rom. 15:19). From this point onwards, Paul's own letters provide documentation of his activities, and the narrative in Acts may be tested by their account. Luke's account directs all of Paul's activity toward Rome and attributes that basic orientation to Paul himself. The book of Acts substantiates this impulse toward Rome by report of two rather mysterious events. These are intended to show that the Spirit of God summoned Paul from the eastern regions of the empire and sent him to the west. Luke's objective is transparent: in recording these events he wishes to demonstrate the inexorable movement toward Rome. His account reads as follows: "And they went through the region of Phrygia and Galatia, having been forbidden by the Holy Spirit to speak the word in Asia. And when they had come opposite Mysia they attempted to go into Bithynia, but the Spirit of Jesus did not allow them" (Acts 16:6–7). Consequently, they went to Troas, the gateway to the west. There—heightening the mystery—Paul had a vision in the night: "A man of Macedonia was standing beseeching him and saying, 'Come over to Macedonia and help us'" (Acts 16:9).

Thus, the Acts of the Apostles presents a "divine redirection" of Paul's mission, drawing him away from Asia and toward the west, beginning with Macedonia and Greece. This representation is clearly influenced by the understanding of church history characteristic of Luke and his Christian community. To Paul himself, however, this turning to the west was part of a planned, progressive fulfillment of his mission to the whole of the then-known world: first to the east, then to the west.

The establishment of a first congregation in Europe, at Philippi in Macedonia, was a source of great joy to Paul. This congregation was to become and remain his favorite. Perhaps he felt especially at home there; but perhaps, even more, his affection for the congregation at Philippi was based on another kind of satisfaction, for it was there that he took the first great step toward the final fulfillment of his eschatological mission: the proclamation of the good news to the west.

The Acts of the Apostles contains another characteristic picture which does not entirely conform to Paul's own view of events. According to the stereotype in Acts, Paul invariably preaches first in the synagogue; only after the Jews have rejected his message does he turn to the Gentiles. This represents the Lukan construction of an authentically Pauline concept: salvation is first for the Jews, then for the Greeks or non-Jews (Rom. 9–11). To Paul, that principle is unassailable. At the Apostolic Council in Jerusalem, however, definite agreements had been made, and Paul subsequently honored them: "(for he who worked through Peter for the mission to the circumcised worked through me also for the Gentiles), and when they had perceived the grace that was given to me, James and Cephas and John, who were reputed to be pillars, gave to me and Barnabas the right hand of fellowship, that we should go to the Gentiles and they to the circumcised" (Gal. 2:8–9). This agreement, however, does not rule out the possibility that Paul did indeed begin his preaching in the synagogues. In synagogue, Paul conducted himself as a *Jew* who proclaimed Christ, and as a Jew he conformed himself to Jewish cultural norms. But it was precisely in the synagogues of the diaspora that he had occasion to meet the "God-fearers," those Gentiles sympathetic to Judaism. In Paul's day, affinity with the spiritual values of Judaism was almost fashionable in many Hellenistic cities. The synagogue therefore provided Paul with an obvious entrée to Gentiles, and, by agency of the God-fearers, to other Gentiles. Thus, reference to preaching in the synagogues must not be taken to imply that Paul initially preached to the Jews and resorted to the Gentiles only after encountering Jewish opposition. That would have been a violation of firm agreements. But more important, Paul was under necessity to preach to the Gentiles, for to Paul, Jesus' death on the cross in itself signified the election of the Gentiles (Gal. 3:13–14).

Not only does the Acts of the Apostles present a highly schematic account of Paul's travels; it also evidences many gaps in information. Only a few are important for the purposes of this review. Meanwhile, we must remember that all the authentic Pauline epistles were written after the Apostolic Council. In the Acts of the Apostles, Luke gives Paul almost complete credit for the expansion of the church after the Apostolic Council. This concentration on the person of Paul has a twofold effect. First, it produces the impression that Pauline congregations constituted the bulk of the ancient church. But the fact is that the largest elements of Christianity, even at that time, were to be found in the east, in Palestine and in eastern and western Syria; there was also an important Christian community in Egypt, though its early history is less well known to us. Second, the book of Acts depicts Paul's labors in a way that tends to reduce his fellow-workers (Barnabas, Silvanus, Timothy, and others) to the status of mere traveling companions, having neither responsibility nor initiative of their own. Titus, a Gentile Christian, is not even mentioned in Acts, despite his strategic role in resolving the difficulties of the Christian community at Corinth. All this serves to heighten the previously mentioned concentration of mission on the person of Paul.

In point of fact, Barnabas, not Paul, was formally invested with leadership of the first missionary journey from Antioch to Cyprus and Cilicia (Acts 13:1–2). To be sure, Paul was always ready to take action when necessary, and ready to assume leadership even in mundane matters (as in the shipwreck off Malta: Acts 28:3) as circumstances required. When brought before the Roman governor at Paphos on Cyprus, Paul appealed to his Roman citizenship for the first time. As a result, the governor quite naturally regarded Paul as the most distinguished of the three traveling companions (Barnabas, Paul, and Barnabas's nephew John Mark). This subtle change in rank and relationship did not escape John Mark. Disillusioned, he ceased collaboration and returned home much to Paul's resentment (Acts 13:13; cf. Acts 15:37–39).

as may the letter to Philemon. Somewhat later, after a resolution of the problems at Corinth, Paul made a joyful journey from Troas to Corinth, where he wrote his epistle to the Romans.

Paul's Reaction in His Letters

The tone of Paul's epistle to the Galatians is extremely harsh. We do not know whether that letter achieved its intended result, but a similarly harsh approach to the situation at Corinth was apparently an almost complete failure (see 2 Cor. 2:1). Afterwards Paul wrote to the Corinthians a letter "with many tears" (2 Cor. 2:4; the tearful letter itself may be incorporated in 2 Cor. 10–13). Then he sent Titus, a Gentile Christian, to Corinth. Titus was apparently more persuasive than Paul himself (2 Cor. 7:5–6, 13:14; 8:6, 16–19, 23; 12:18). Meanwhile, Paul was forced to leave Ephesus. In Macedonia, he anxiously awaited Titus's arrival. At last, Titus reported the success of his mission in Corinth (2 Cor. 2:6; 7:5–16). Paul was highly gratified by this development, as attested by his fourth letter to the Corinthians (a letter which may be contained, at least in fragments, in 2 Cor. 2:1–13). He proceeded with great joy to Corinth.

Apart from some residual problems in Ephesus, Paul could look back from Corinth on an eminently successful career. This is attested by the letter written from Corinth to Rome. The epistle is a preparation for the intended inauguration of the second phase of Paul's apostolate. It provides a thematization of the gospel he had carried to the eastern half of the empire, his first and now finally cultivated field of labor (Rom. 15:23–24). In the epistle to the Romans, Paul considers the current issues of faith in a detached, objective manner, and we are made aware of his intention to preach *this* gospel in Spain, the westernmost outpost of the empire (Rom. 15:24–28).

All this suggests that Paul's major epistles are not mere recapitulations of the message first preached to nascent congregations in the course of the apostolic journeys. The letters are a penetrating, actualizing interpretation of that message, written out of the experience of the recent problems.

If we wish to recover the message preached by Paul in establishing his key congregations, we must look to the first epistle to the Thessalonians. There we may find at least the substance of his original proclamation, together with a kind of schema of the primitive Christian proclamation to the Gentiles. Its points include: belief in one God; belief in the judgment of the unrepentant; and eschatological hope for all who turn to Christ (1 Thess. 1:9–19; cf. Acts 14:15; 17:22–31; Heb. 6:1–2). We must beware, however, of taking this schema to mean that Paul summoned the Gentiles first to a generalized religious monotheism and then subsumed the Christ-event under that general conception of God. Paul states: " . . . You turned to God from idols, to serve a living and true God, and to wait for his Son from heaven, whom he raised from the dead, Jesus who delivers us from the wrath to come" (1 Thess. 1:9–10).

"The living and true God," an expression current in the intertestamental literature, was adopted by early Christians (Acts 14:15; Mt. 16:16; 1 Tim. 3:15; Heb. 3:12, etc.). But in using this expression, Paul typically speaks also of "Jesus": Jesus, the historical person, is the Risen

One, "the Lord Jesus" (as also in Rom. 10:9 and 1 Cor. 12:3). The name "Jesus" is directly linked with the resurrection (Rom. 8:11; 2 Cor. 4:14; 2 Cor. 4:10–11). To Paul, the awaited Son of God is the historical man Jesus. Therefore, acceptance of the one true God (monotheism) is invested with a Christian content from the very beginning. Paul's fundamental message is based on his expectation of the return of Jesus, the risen Son of God, as Savior. Paul's proclamation is focused on God; it is divine service; through God's Son, the risen Jesus, it offers the hope of salvation in the impending judgment.

It may be necessary for us to remind ourselves that in the late first and early second centuries, the "legendary Paul"—his name and fame—were better known than were his letters. The Acts of the Apostles neither cites nor mentions any of Paul's epistles. His authority and the agitations of his opponents were known by reputation, and not from his own writings. The Paul-tradition antedated the dissemination of his letters and, in the first century, was more important than the letters themselves. The authors of the *Epistle of Barnabas* and the *Didache* (a manual of instruction probably dating from the early second century) were apparently unacquainted with any of the Pauline writings; so were Papias and Justin. Interest in Paul's epistles and acquaintance with them become evident only with Irenaeus, Clement of Alexandria, and Origen.

The Problem of Asia

This stormy period was at the same time the height of Paul's literary activity. Only afterwards was Paul able to go to Jerusalem to deliver the collections of his predominantly Greek congregations. Once he had completed that delivery, he intended to pursue his plan to journey via Rome to Spain.

The Acts of the Apostles rather innocuously reports that Paul "sailed past Ephesus" on the voyage to Jerusalem, ostensibly to save time (Acts 20:16). But then we are told that he sent messengers back to Ephesus to invite the leaders of the congregation there (Luke refers to them by the non-Pauline term "presbyters"; RSV "elders") to attend him at Miletus for a final farewell (Acts 20:17). The account is somewhat forced and deliberately obscures any problems. Still, its very obscurity provides some insight into the so-called "Apostolic Testament" which Paul purportedly delivered to the church leaders of Asia. This Lukan account of Paul's last farewell to the Ephesians (Acts 20:28–38) portrays what is for Paul a painful, present reality as a threatening future event: "I [Paul] know that after my departure fierce wolves will come in among you, not sparing the flock; and from among your own selves will arise men speaking perverse things, to draw away the disciples after them" (Acts 20:29–30). That, however, is precisely the situation which Paul himself has already described (2 Cor. 1:8–9). Moreover, in Romans 16:17–20, Paul gives greeting to a number of people, all of whom reside in Ephesus, then suddenly changes his tone to one of sharp admonition. This would make no sense in a letter written to a congregation as unfamiliar to him as was the church in Rome. Consequently, many exegetes regard the passage as a fragment of an authentic letter, originally sent by Paul to

Ephesus: "I appeal to you, brethren, to take note of those who create dissensions and difficulties, in opposition to the doctrine you have been taught; avoid them" (Rom. 16:17). It seems likely that this describes the situation which caused Paul to bypass Ephesus. The later, deutero-Pauline literature will attribute to Paul this sentiment: "You are aware that all who are in Asia turned against me" (2 Tim. 1:15). And the first epistle to Timothy states: "As I urged you when I was going to Macedonia, remain at Ephesus that you may charge certain persons not to teach any different doctrine, nor to occupy themselves with myths and endless genealogies" (1 Tim. 1:3–4a). This may shed light on the unsatisfactory conclusion of Paul's visit in Ephesus after his departure for Macedonia (see Acts 20:16–17). The deutero-Pauline epistles, though written much later, appear to connect with earlier problems. What were the specific problems that impelled Paul to leave Ephesus and later to avoid the city? The report of the uproar caused by the silversmiths at Ephesus (Acts 19:23–40), whose trade in amulets and shrines had been adversely affected by Christian abjuration of the Artemis cult, dates from the earliest days of the mission at Ephesus. It cannot have been the reason for Paul's later avoidance of the city. The appeal to lack of time (Acts 20:16) is also unsatisfactory, for Paul immediately made time for a stop at Miletus. We do not know the immediate cause of the difficulties (see 2 Tim. 2:18). We do know, however, that Pauline Christianity gained ground less quickly after the death of Paul. We also know that the Pauline movement came into more frequent contact with other Christian traditions, and that Paulinism was ultimately supplanted in Asia. Authentic Paulinism eventually came off second best, even in those congregations whose origin and orientation had been thoroughly Pauline. It seems that other traditions, with different approaches to Christian experience, proved more congenial to the Asian soul. It is noteworthy, from a historical point of view, that Ephesus (together with Alexandria) became a primary locus for the later rediscovery of the Johannine corpus. Outside Macedonia and Greece, the western provinces of Asia Minor had been Paul's largest field of endeavor. Ultimately, however, they showed more affinity for other, headier forms of Christianity. The deutero-Pauline epistles, especially Colossians and Ephesians, may be the harbingers of this trend; or perhaps they are a reaction to it, made in the name and spirit of Paul.

The Deutero-Pauline (Post-Pauline) Epistles

The deutero-Pauline movement presupposes the death of Paul. Not only could the composition of pseudonymous epistles by later Pauline leaders occur only after the death of him in whose name they were written; it was only after Paul's death that there arose in Pauline circles a concern to collect his letters. The authority which Paul enjoyed at the time—to say nothing of the suspicion and opposition he encountered from the "official church"—was by no means based on his letters (which had not yet been "published"), but on his reputation, the *fama Pauli*. Sometime after Paul's death, his disciples began to collect and promulgate his letters. This presupposed a certain redactional process, and that process exerted its own significant influence, even on the authentic epistles. The deutero-Pauline movement arose as a direct result of the publication of the authentic Pauline epistles. After Paul's death, new letters, written in Paul's name, began to surface in Pauline circles. These are the so-called deutero-Pauline epistles: Colossians, Ephesians, 2 Thessalonians, and the Pastoral epistles.

Given the lively commerce which flowed between the major cities of the time, the Pauline congregations inevitably came into contact with other forms and traditions of Christianity. In time, these other schools produced their own religious documents (the Gospels according to Mark, Matthew, and John; Luke-Acts; Revelation). There was also the so-called official church, which based its practice not on the writing of any particular circle, but on Jesus-traditions and a Christian interpretation of the Greek Old Testament. The deutero-Pauline movement, deriving from Paul's disciples, evolved in various ways. The epistles to the Colossians and Ephesians bear witness to a deutero-Paulinism different from that of the Pastoral epistles. The latter, in turn, differ from 2 Thessalonians.

After A. D. 70, the center of Christianity in western Asia Minor shifted to Ephesus. The Pauline Christianity planted there was thrust into contact with other Christian traditions. In order to understand the situation, we must remember that the Hellenism of Asia Minor was more strongly colored by oriental influences than the Hellenism of Macedonia and other western provinces. Asia Minor, while maintaining its own distinctive social fabric, was a melting pot of eastern and western cultures. The oriental, Asiatic disposition yearned for dramatic experiences of intrapsychic, pneumatic fulfillment. To the people of these regions, the sense of living in a world populated by angels and demons posed an existential problem of great magnitude. Beneficent spirits were believed to impel every human good deed. Behind every evil deed, there lurked malevolent, demonic principalities or cosmic powers. Protection against these evil forces was sought in various religious rites. Astrology and calendrical calculations, depending on reckonings from moonrise or sunrise, were part and parcel of daily life. Horoscopes were actively consulted. The people of Asia Minor were in search of a *way*, a philosophy of life. They were open to every offer of a means to cope with the world.

We have indicated above that Paul, in his missionary travels, intended to establish Christian communities in the major cities. This ecclesial strategy was based on the assumption that the congregations thus formed would in turn function as missionary centers, spreading Pauline Christianity throughout their respective regions. Any congregation established according to this plan, whether by Paul himself or by one of his missionary centers, could accurately be termed a *Pauline* community. Paul was the authority for all these congregations.

This reality made it possible, after Paul's death, for church leaders old and new to assert and legitimize their authority—especially in the Pauline congregations—by emphasizing their fervent desire to maintain and further the work and gospel of Paul. When these leaders, on their own initiative, wrote letters to their congregations, the letters were supplied with the name of the great Apostle, the tradition-bearer and pioneer of the community. Such pseudonymity was a widespread practice in Antiquity. We may now more clearly assess the basic intention of these letters. The so-called deutero-Pauline epistles intend to continue the apostolic tradition of Paul; they build further on the apostolic foundation which he laid.

The so-called Pastoral epistles (1 and 2 Timothy, Titus) reflect the very essence of deutero-Pauline principles. They are primarily concerned not with an unbroken succession in office but with an unabridged succession in the doctrine of the Pauline apostolic tradition: "And what you have heard from me before many witnesses entrust to faithful men who will be able to teach it to others also" (2 Tim. 2:2). The self-understanding of the post-Pauline leadership permits them to place this sentiment on Paul's own lips, and not without warrant. The succession at stake here is clearly the succession of the *Pauline* gospel. Paul received this gospel from God (1 Tim. 1:11; cf. 1 Cor. 3:9). Paul himself transmitted it to Titus and Timothy (1 Tim. 6:20; 2 Tim. 1:13–14), and these in turn were to convey this liberating gospel to others (2 Tim. 2:2). It is an "entrusted deposit" of truth (1 Tim. 6:20; 2 Tim. 1:14). This entrusted deposit is "the gospel" (2 Tim. 1:11; also 2 Tim. 2:8), but the gospel as Paul construed it (2 Tim. 1:11–14). In the Pastoral letters, this Pauline interpretation of the gospel is called the *didaskalia* ("doctrine": 1 Tim. 1:10; 2 Tim. 4:3; Tit. 1:9; 2:1), that is, "the doctrine of God our Savior" (Tit. 2:10). In the deutero-Pauline epistles, Paul himself is the great *didaskalos*, the teacher of the divine gospel (1 Tim. 2:7; 2 Tim. 1:11).

The appeal to "Paulinism" had inherent limitations. These became evident when the Pauline congregations were confronted not only with other approaches to Christianity but also with certain forms of cosmic-mythical religious impulse which apparently infiltrated the Pauline communities.

This is especially true of the period following the death of Paul—indeed, Paul had already had to deal with the problem in his last year in Ephesus—when the Pauline congregations in Asia sustained a severe challenge. Paul's own letter to the Galatians would suggest that the Judaizers who had formerly dogged his path were not a major factor in the crisis. More important was the fact that Judaism itself was held in high esteem by the Gentiles of Asia Minor. This high regard for Judaism coalesced with the cosmic, mystical religious traditions of Asia Minor to produce a syncretistic blend. To judge from the epistle to the Galatians, Paul may have failed to perceive the real nature of the problem; he attributes it to his earlier experience of Jewish-Christian opposition to the "Pauline gospel." Deutero-Paulinism is a product of third-generation Christians.

Paul, Israel, and Jesus of Nazareth

At some point after the first missionary journey, Paul and Barnabas were seized with resolve to lay their gospel before the esteemed leaders in Jerusalem. This decision was precipitated by the fact that certain conservative Jewish Christians from Jerusalem had made a visit to the congregation in Antioch. Their report to Jerusalem was apparently detrimental to Paul and Barnabas. Did Paul go to Jerusalem on his own initiative, or was he summoned there by the pillars of the Jerusalem church? Paul himself says only that he went "by revelation" (Gal. 2:2). In either case, then, he understood it as the will of God. And he deliberately took with him Titus, a Gentile Christian.

Paul felt no personal need to have his gospel approved by men, for he had received it from God (Gal. 1:11–12, 15–20). In the epistle to the Galatians, he provides a detailed account of the Apostolic Council in Jerusalem. He states: "... I laid before them (but privately before those who were of repute) the gospel which I preach among the Gentiles, lest somehow I should be running or had run in vain" (Gal. 2:2). Thus, he feared that without the recognition of the pillars in Jerusalem (James, Cephas, and John), all his past efforts might be fruitless and without effect. This means that his real fear was of a definitive breach between the Gentile and Jewish constituencies of the church. To be sure, there were strong differences of emphasis in the viewpoints of those two groups within the "church of God"; yet Paul, for his part, saw the two entities as part of "the one congregation" or assembly of God. If, on the other hand, this view was not shared by the Jerusalem congregation, then Paul had labored in vain for his ideal of a unified though pluriform church. It is this unity, and not Paul's gospel *as such*, which required confirmation by the leaders of the Jerusalem church. Unity demands *mutual* recognition. This was solemnly conferred by the Apostolic Council: "... They perceived the grace that was given to me ..." (Gal. 2:9a); and that recognition was sealed with the solemn "right hand of fellowship" (Gal. 2:9).

As it happened, certain Jewish Christians did not heartily endorse this solemn handclasp. Paul calls them "false brethren" (Gal. 2:4). Moving out from Jerusalem and Judea, they generated manifold difficulties for the Pauline movement. By and large, however, the Greek-speaking Jews of the diaspora could relate more easily to Paul's viewpoint; for as Jews of the diaspora, they too adopted a critical stance toward the law and the temple (see Acts 6:13). But these Christian "Hellenists" had been forced to flee Jerusalem. As a result, the congregation there was composed entirely of Jewish Christians (the so-called "Hebrews"), who continued to visit the temple and maintained a high regard for the Torah. Their Christology was primarily a Messianic Christology of the Coming One; and they constituted a religious grouping within Israel, alongside the Pharisees, Sadducees, and Essenes. In the beginning, this community was not molested by the Jewish authorities, for belief in a particular person as the Messiah has never been a heresy in Judaism.

Paul's fundamental premise was quite different from theirs. He believed that by Jesus' action the salvation promised to Israel was made accessible even to non-Jews. Moreover, contrary to Jewish proselytism, Paul held that Gentiles need not first become Jews in order to attain salvation: they were free from the law and circumcision. Paulinism proclaims that those who were "far from the salvation of the Jews" have been "brought near" in Christ. The one God is not the God of only one people; he embraces all men and women and all nations, and the consequence of that embrace must be reconciliation among individuals and nations. Universal love does not permit exclusion of one's fellow from the community. To do so would be to Paul a contradiction of the "truth of the gospel" (Gal. 2:14).

It was much more difficult for Gentile Christians to raise this issue than it was for a Christian Jew like Paul. But there was always the danger that Paul's fellow Jews would regard him as an apostate. After all, Saul himself had at first violently persecuted the Christians, and precisely because he regarded the Jesus-movement as apostasy from Judaism. His conversion to belief in Christ therefore involved at the same time a new view of Israel and a sending to the Gentiles (Gal. 3:6–14). For Paul as an orthodox Jew and a Pharisee, the *Torah*, the law, was the embodiment of God's definitive grace toward the Jewish nation and, through Israel, to all humankind; for Paul as a Christian Jew, God's unique and definitive grace toward the Jewish nation is embodied in the *promise to Abraham*, through which all the nations of the earth are to be blessed (Gal. 3:6–14; Rom. 4:1–25). It is a truly Jewish conception, with radical consequences. Both of God's great promises to Israel are fully honored, but at the same time the ultimate value of the Torah is diminished and, in practice, often set aside. In Paul's view, Christ realizes God's promises to the Jews and at the same time removes the "fence," the protective enclosure (Bar. 3:9–4:4), which bars the Gentiles from access to Israel's salvation. To many sincere Jews even today, such a notion is intolerable and constitutes nothing less than apostasy. The idea in itself is seen as a breach with Judaism.

To accuse Paul of anti-Semitism is nonsense; there is no historical warrant for such a suggestion. It is true, however, that Christians on the basis of their reading of Paul and other New Testament texts introduced a *Christian variant* into the widespread anti-Semitism of the time. Christendom must bear the guilt of this development, which intensified in the course of western history, generating the horrors perpetrated against the Jewish people in the Middle Ages. But Christians must also acknowledge guilt for the shameful silence of most Christians and the official church in the face of what was inflicted on millions of Jews in our own history and, indeed, before our very eyes. For these reasons, Paulinism poses acute problems in the dialogue between Christians and Jews. It presents a challenge to both Christians and Jews, at least if Christians are willing to bring to such dialogue a consciousness of their own sins against the Jewish people.

For Paul, there exists a tension between his *being in Christ* and his *being a Jew*. This can be resolved only in the mystery of God; Paul does not achieve a coherent theological solution (Rom. 11:25, 33–36). Paulinism does not create an ecclesiastical *tertium genus* in which Jews and non-Jews must relinquish their particularity; yet it asserts: "There is neither Jew nor Greek ... in Christ Jesus" (Gal. 3:28), and " ... in Christ Jesus neither circumcision nor uncircumcision is of any avail, but faith working through love" (Gal. 5:6). The church, consisting of Jews and non-Jews, has become "the Israel of God" (Gal. 6:16). In reality, however, this church became almost exclusively a Gentile church. According to Paul, the Jewish people continued to constitute only the "Israel according to the flesh" (1 Cor. 10:18 RSVm). "Christ redeemed us from the curse of the law" (Gal. 3:13), but only so that " ... in Christ Jesus the blessing of Abraham might come upon the Gentiles" (Gal. 3:14). For Paul it was a matter of freedom, not uniformity, in the "church of God." As we have seen, his missionary code was one of non-interference with other Christian traditions, including the Jewish-Christian tradition with its reverence for the Torah and the Temple. But the present reality is quite different from Paul's ideal, for today a Gentile church stands over against *non-Christian* Judaism.

The Jewish creed remained Paul's fundamental creed: "Hear, O Israel: the Lord our God is one LORD; and you shall love the LORD your God with all your heart, and with all your soul, and with all your might" (Deut. 6:4). But Paul asks: " . . . Is God the God of Jews only? Is he not the God of Gentiles also?" (Rom. 3:29). Here Paul draws out the radical consequence of Jewish monotheism. His relativization of the law and of every legalistic system—not only that of Judaism (see Rom. 7:11–14, 22)—is intimately connected with his belief in God in Jesus Christ: " . . . We hold that a man is justified by faith apart from works of law" (Rom. 3:28). The true heart of Paulinism may be traced to the statement which the gospel attributes to Jesus himself: "Woe to you, scribes and Pharisees, hypocrites! for you tithe mint and dill and cummin, and have negated the weightier matters of the law, justice and mercy and faith" (Mt. 23:23). Neither Jesus nor Paul directs his point against the law as such, but against autarchic compliance with the law. Thus Paul's proclamation, albeit in a different, polemical situation, is the same as the proclamation of Jesus of Nazareth, who announced the kingdom of God to the poor, the outcast, the powerless—to any willing to open themselves to God's "kingdom and his righteousness" (Mt. 6:33). Both Jesus and Paul were concerned with the "glorious liberty" (Rom. 8:21) of the children of God. Furthermore, Jesus had originally aligned himself with the preaching of John the Baptist and had proclaimed that circumcision offered no guarantee of salvation: " . . . God is able from these stones to raise up children to Abraham" (Lk. 3:8). This was an understanding quite in line with traditional Jewish thinking, at least as represented in the Deuteronomic understanding of history. Jewish Essenism also expressed the same basic criticism of Israel, as we learn from the discoveries at Qumran.

In the heat of polemic, Paul naturally let hard words fall, especially against Jewish Christians. In what was apparently his last epistle, he expressed himself freely concerning the relation of Israel and the church: "For I could wish that I myself were accursed and cut off from Christ for the sake of my brethren, my kinsmen by race" (Rom. 9:9). The election of Israel and its ultimate salvation remained beyond any doubt. "God has not rejected his people" (Rom. 11:2). The Gentiles are only the "wild shoot" grafted into the noble, fruitful olive tree of Israel (Rom. 11:16–24). Paul dares to proclaim what seems impossible: " . . . We preach Christ crucified, a stumbling block to Jews and folly to Gentiles, but to those who are called, both Jews and Greeks, Christ the power of God and the wisdom of God" (1 Cor. 1:23–24). For both Jews and Greeks, it is a difficult thing to be a Christian. Still, Paul believes it is less foreign to the Jews: "For if you have been cut from what is by nature a wild olive tree, and grafted, contrary to nature, into a cultivated olive tree, how much more will these natural branches be grafted back into their own olive tree" (Rom. 11:24).

For contemporary Judaism it is not Jesus himself, but the Christ confessed by Christians who remains a "stumbling block," and all the more because of all that history has inflicted on the Jews in the name of belief in Christ. Many Jews conclude that Jesus Christ is necessary for Gentiles, but not for Jews, who already have access to the Father. Other Jews accept Jesus as a prophet of the kingdom of God and an advocate of the poor and oppressed; some even accept Jesus as a Jewish critic of his own Jewish religiosity. And some Jews are fascinated by Jesus, as one is by the mystery of one's own brother. But to believe in Jesus as the salvation of all humankind or to give credence to the high Christology of the church is considered incompatible with Jewish identity.

A particular problem is presented by certain Christian theories of the atonement. That God's love should demand the sacrifice of his Son is to many Jews (and not only to them) a contradiction of the lesson learned from the test of Abraham: "Human sacrifice is an abomination to me" (see Lev. 18:21–30 and 20:1–5). "For I desire steadfast love and not sacrifice, the knowledge of God rather than burnt offerings" (Hos. 6:6; cf. Isa. 1:11–17). Some Christian interpretations of what is rightly called Jesus' expiatory death are not only un-Jewish, but unbiblical as well. The cross was not devised by God, but by sinful men. Their purpose simply failed to thwart God's purpose.

This way of viewing the cross is especially important when we consider the question posed by Martin Buber in an address published in 1952: "In this our own time, one asks again and again: how is Jewish life still possible after Auschwitz? I would like to frame the question more correctly: how is a life with God still possible in a time in which there is an Auschwitz? The estrangement has become too cruel, the hiddenness too deep."* Why does God hide his face? (Job 13:24). It is necessary for us to rethink our Christian theology of a triumphalistic, almighty God, and to do so particularly in the light of the Christ-event and the most profound themes of Paulinism: God's power "is made perfect in weakness" (2 Cor. 12:9; see also Rom. 8:26; 2 Cor. 4:7; 13:4). All Christians must live with this reality: "But we have this treasure in earthen vessels, to show that the transcendent power belongs to God and not to us" (2 Cor. 4:7).

* Martin Buber, "The Dialogue between Heaven and Earth," trans. by I. M. Lask, in *On Judaism*, ed. by Nahum A. Glatzer (New York: Schocken Books, 1967), p. 224.

PAUL,
a servant of Jesus Christ, called to be an apostle, set apart for the gospel of God Rom 1:1

For this reason, I, Paul, [am] a prisoner for Christ Jesus on behalf of you Gentiles .... Of this gospel I was made a minister according to the gift of God's grace which was given me by the working of his power. To me, though I am the very least of all the saints, this grace was given, to preach to the Gentiles the unsearchable riches of Christ, and to make all men see what is the plan of the mystery hidden for ages in God who created all things; that through the church the manifold wisdom of God might now be made known to the principalities and powers in the heavenly places. EPH 3:1, 7–10

Now many signs and wonders were done among the people by the hands of the apostles .... so that they even carried out the sick into the streets, and laid them on beds and pallets, that as Peter came by at least his shadow might fall on some of them. The people also gathered from the towns around Jerusalem, bringing the sick and those afflicted with unclean spirits, and they were all healed. ACTS 5:12, 15–16

And the word of God increased; and the number of the disciples multiplied greatly in Jerusalem, and a great many of the priests were obedient to the faith.

Right: (1) Paul
On the following four pages:
(2) The seven-branched candelabrum
(3) Stephen is led away to be stoned
(4) The Stephen Gate in the east wall of Jerusalem
(5) The stoning of Stephen

And Stephen, full of grace and power, did great wonders and signs among the people. Then some of those who belonged to the synagogue of the Freedmen (as it was called), and of the Cyrenians, and of the Alexandrians, and of those from Cilicia and Asia, arose and disputed with Stephen. But they could not withstand the wisdom and the Spirit with which he spoke.... And they stirred up the people and the elders and the scribes, and they came upon him and seized him and brought him before the council.

ACTS 6:7, 8–10, 12

And Stephen said: ... "You stiff-necked people, uncircumcised in heart and ears, you always resist the Holy Spirit. As your fathers did, so do you. Which of the prophets did not your fathers persecute? And they killed those who announced beforehand the coming of the Righteous One, whom you have now betrayed and murdered, you who received the law as delivered by angels and did not keep it."

Now when they heard these things they were enraged, and they ground their teeth against him. ACTS 7:1, 51–54

But he, full of the Holy Spirit, gazed into heaven and saw the glory of God, and Jesus standing at the right hand of God; and he said, "Behold, I see the heavens opened, and the Son of man standing at the right hand of God." But they cried out with a loud voice and stopped their ears and rushed together upon him. Then they cast him out of the city and stoned him; and the witnesses laid down their garments at the feet of a young man named Saul. And as they were stoning Stephen, he prayed, "Lord Jesus, receive my spirit." And he knelt down and cried with a loud voice, "Lord, do not hold this sin against them." And when he had said this, he fell asleep.

And Saul was consenting to his death.

And on that day a great persecution arose against the church in Jerusalem; and they were all scattered throughout the region of Judea and Samaria, except the apostles.

Devout men buried Stephen, and made great lamentation over him.

But Saul was ravaging the church, and entering house after house, he dragged off men and women and committed them to prison.

ACTS 7:55–60; 8:1–3

On the preceding two pages:
(6) Burial chambers on Mount Zion
(7) High priests
Left: (8) Stairway of the Temple of Augustus in Samaria

[Paul later said of this time and his conversion:]

"I am a Jew, born at Tarsus in Cilicia, but brought up in this city at the feet of Gamaliel, educated according to the strict manner of the law of our fathers, being zealous for God as you all are this day. I persecuted this Way to the death, binding and delivering to prison both men and women, as the high priest and the whole council of elders bear me witness. From them I received letters to the brethren, and I journeyed to Damascus to take those also who were there and bring them in bonds to Jerusalem to be punished.

ACTS 22:3–5

"As I made my journey and drew near to Damascus, about noon a great light from heaven suddenly shone about me. And I fell to the ground and heard a voice saying to me, 'Saul, Saul, why do you persecute me?' And I answered, 'Who are you, Lord?' And he said to me, 'I am Jesus of Nazareth whom you are persecuting.' Now those who were with me saw the light but did not hear the voice of the one who was speaking to me. And I said, 'What shall I do, Lord?' And the Lord said to me, 'Rise, and go into Damascus, and there you will be told all that is appointed for you to do.' And when I could not see because of the brightness of that light, I was led by the hand by those who were with me, and came into Damascus.

"And one Ananias, a devout man according to the law, well spoken of by all the Jews who lived there, came to me, and standing by me said to me, 'Brother Saul, receive your sight.' And in that very hour I received my sight and saw him. And he said, 'The God of our fathers appointed you to know his will, to see the Just One and to hear a voice from his mouth; for you will be a witness for him to all men of what you have seen and heard. And now why do you wait? Rise and be baptized, and wash away your sins, calling on his name.' "

ACTS 22:6–16

For several days he was with the disciples at Damascus. And in the synagogues immediately he proclaimed Jesus, saying, "He is the Son of God." And all who heard him were amazed, and said, "Is not this the man who made havoc in Jerusalem of those who called on this name? And he has come here for this purpose, to bring them bound before the chief priests." But Saul increased all the more in strength, and confounded the Jews who lived in Damascus by proving that Jesus was the Christ.

When many days had passed, the Jews plotted to kill him, but their plot became known to Saul. They were watching the gates day and night, to kill him; but his disciples took him by night and let him down over the wall, lowering him in a basket.

ACTS 9:19–25

Right: (9) Paul
On the following four pages:
(10) The Damascus Road
(11) The conversion of Paul   (12) Paul's flight from Damascus   (13) The wilderness of Judaea

DIMISSVS·E·IN·S

[Paul reported on the period following his conversion in the letter to the Galatians:]

But when he who had set me apart before I was born, and had called me through his grace, was pleased to reveal his Son to me, in order that I might preach him among the Gentiles, I did not confer with flesh and blood, nor did I go up to Jerusalem to those who were apostles before me, but I went away into Arabia; and again I returned to Damascus. Then after three years I went up to Jerusalem to visit Cephas, and remained with him fifteen days.   GAL 1:15–18

And when he [Paul] had come to Jerusalem he attempted to join the disciples; and they were all afraid of him, for they did not believe that he was a disciple. But Barnabas took him, and brought him to the apostles, and declared to them how on the road he had seen the Lord, who spoke to him, and how at Damascus he had preached boldly in the name of Jesus. So he went in and out among them at Jerusalem, preaching boldly in the name of the Lord. And he spoke and disputed against the Hellenists; but they were seeking to kill him. And when the brethren knew it, they brought him down to Caesarea, and sent him off to Tarsus.   ACTS 9:26–30

Now those who were scattered because of the persecution that arose over Stephen traveled as far as Phoenicia and Cyprus and Antioch, speaking the word to none except Jews. But there were some of them, men of Cyprus and Cyrene, who on coming to Antioch spoke to the Greeks also, preaching the Lord Jesus. And the hand of the Lord was with them, and a great number that believed turned to the Lord.

News of this came to the ears of the church in Jerusalem, and they sent Barnabas to Antioch. When he came and saw the grace of God, he was glad; and he exhorted them all to remain faithful to the Lord with steadfast purpose; for he was a good man, full of the Holy Spirit and of faith. And a large company was added to the Lord.

So Barnabas went to Tarsus to look for Saul; and when he had found him, he brought him to Antioch. For a whole year they met with the church, and taught a large company of people; and in Antioch the disciples were for the first time called Christians.   ACTS 11:19–26

On the preceding two pages:
(14) Peter and Paul
Left: (15) Remains of the city gate of Tarsus

The First Missionary Journey

Now in the church at Antioch there were prophets and teachers, Barnabas, Simeon who was called Niger, Lucius of Cyrene, Manaen a member of the court of Herod the tetrarch, and Saul. While they were worshiping the Lord and fasting, the Holy Spirit said, "Set apart for me Barnabas and Saul for the work to which I have called them." Then after fasting and praying they laid their hands on them and sent them off.

So, being sent out by the Holy Spirit, they went down to Seleucia; and from there they sailed to Cyprus. When they arrived at Salamis, they proclaimed the word of God in the synagogues of the Jews. And they had John to assist them. When they had gone through the whole island as far as Paphos, they came upon a certain magician, a Jewish false prophet, named Bar-Jesus. He was with the proconsul, Sergius Paulus, a man of intelligence, who summoned Barnabas and Saul and sought to hear the word of God. But Elymas the magician (for that is the meaning of his name) withstood them, seeking to turn away the proconsul from the faith.

But Saul, who is also called Paul, filled with the Holy Spirit, looked intently at him and said, "You son of the devil, you enemy of all righteousness, full of all deceit and villainy, will you not stop making crooked the straight paths of the Lord? And now, behold, the hand of the Lord is upon you, and you shall be blind and unable to see the sun for a time." Immediately mist and darkness fell upon him and he went about seeking people to lead him by the hand.

Then the proconsul believed, when he saw what had occurred, for he was astonished at the teaching of the Lord. ACTS 13:1–12

Now Paul and his company set sail from Paphos, and came to Perga in Pamphylia. And John left them and returned to Jerusalem; but they passed on from Perga and came to Antioch of Pisidia. ACTS 13:13–14

Right: (16) The Orontes River near Antioch
On the following four pages:
(17) Ship of the Roman period
(18) The Roman forum in Salamis on Cyprus
(19) Peter and Paul
(20) Roman Governor

PAVSV
CRITO
VS

And on the sabbath day they went into the synagogue and sat down. After the reading of the law and the prophets, the rulers of the synagogue sent to them, saying, "Brethren, if you have any word of exhortation for the people, say it."

So Paul stood up, and motioning with his hand said: "Men of Israel, and you that fear God, listen. The God of this people Israel chose our fathers and made the people great during their stay in the land of Egypt, and with uplifted arm he led them out of it. And for about forty years he bore with them in the wilderness. And when he had destroyed seven nations in the land of Canaan, he gave them their land as an inheritance, for about four hundred and fifty years. And after that he gave them judges until Samuel the prophet. Then they asked for a king; and God gave them Saul the son of Kish, a man of the tribe of Benjamin, for forty years. And when he had removed him, he raised up David to be their king; of whom he testified and said, 'I have found in David the son of Jesse a man after my heart, who will do all my will.' Of this man's posterity God has brought to Israel a Savior, Jesus, as he promised. Before his coming John had preached a baptism of repentance to all the people of Israel. And as John was finishing his course, he said, 'What do you suppose that I am? I am not he. No, but after me one is coming, the sandals of whose feet I am not worthy to untie.'

"Brethren, sons of the family of Abraham, and those among you that fear God, to us has been sent the message of this salvation. For those who live in Jerusalem and their rulers, because they did not recognize him nor understand the utterances of the prophets which are read every sabbath, fulfilled these by condemning him. Though they could charge him with nothing deserving death, yet they asked Pilate to have him killed. And when they had fulfilled all that was written of him, they took him down from the tree, and laid him in a tomb. But God raised him from the dead; and for many days he appeared to those who came up with him from Galilee to Jerusalem, who are now his witnesses to the people.

"And we bring you the good news that what God promised to the fathers, this he has fulfilled to us their children by raising Jesus .... Let it be known to you therefore, brethren, that through this man forgiveness of sins is proclaimed to you, and by him every one that believes is freed from everything from which you could not be freed by the law of Moses.

"Beware, therefore, lest there come upon you what is said in the prophets: 'Behold, you scoffers, and wonder, and perish; for I do a deed in your days, a deed you will never believe, if one declares it to you.'"

ACTS 13:14–33, 38–41

On the preceding two pages:
(21) The Bay of Atallia
(22) Remains of a gate tower in Perga
Left: (23) Aqueduct in Antioch in Pisidia

As they went out, the people begged that these things might be told them the next sabbath. And when the meeting of the synagogue broke up, many Jews and devout converts to Judaism followed Paul and Barnabas, who spoke to them and urged them to continue in the grace of God.

The next sabbath almost the whole city gathered together to hear the word of God. But when the Jews saw the multitudes, they were filled with jealousy, and contradicted what was spoken by Paul, and reviled him. And Paul and Barnabas spoke out boldly, saying, "It was necessary that the word of God should be spoken first to you. Since you thrust it from you, and judge yourselves unworthy of eternal life, behold, we turn to the Gentiles. For so the Lord has commanded us, saying: 'I have set you to be a light for the Gentiles, that you may bring salvation to the uttermost parts of the earth.'"

And when the Gentiles heard this, they were glad and glorified the word of God; and as many as were ordained to eternal life believed. And the word of the Lord spread throughout all the region.

But the Jews incited the devout women of high standing and the leading men of the city, and stirred up persecution against Paul and Barnabas, and drove them out of their district. But they shook off the dust from their feet against them, and went to Iconium.

Now at Iconium they entered together into the Jewish synagogue, and so spoke that a great company believed, both of Jews and of Greeks.   ACTS 13:42–51; 14:1

And a man named Onesiphorus, who had heard that Paul was come to Iconium, went out with his children Simmias and Zeno and his wife Lectra to meet Paul, that he might receive him to his house .... And when Paul was entered into the house of Onesiphorus there was great joy, and bowing of the knees and breaking of bread, and the word of God concerning continence and the resurrection.

And while Paul was thus speaking in the midst of the assembly in the house of Onesiphorus, a virgin (named) Thecla, who was betrothed to a man (named) Thamyris, sat at a near-by window and listened night and day to the word of the virgin life as it was spoken by Paul; and she did not turn away from the window, but pressed on in the faith rejoicing exceedingly.

And Thamyris stood before the judgment-seat and cried aloud: "Proconsul, this man—we know not whence he is—who does not allow maidens to marry, let him declare before thee for what cause he teaches these things." ... But the governor was not easily to be swayed, and he called Paul, saying to him: "Who art thou, and what dost thou teach? For it is no light accusation that they bring against thee."

Right: (24) Ruins of a synagogue — On the following four pages: (25) Paul in disputation with Greeks and Jews   (26) Paul under threat   (27) View of the citadel of Iconium

And Paul lifted up his voice and said: "If I today am examined as to what I teach, then listen, Proconsul. The living God, the God of vengeance, the jealous God, the God who has need of nothing, has sent me since he desires the salvation of men, that I may draw them away from corruption and impurity, all pleasure and death, that they may sin no more. For this cause God sent His own Son, whom I preach and teach that in him men have hope, who alone had compassion upon a world in error; that men may no longer be under judgment but have faith, and fear of God, and knowledge of propriety, and love of truth. If then I teach the things revealed to me by God, what wrong do I do, Proconsul?"

When the governor heard this, he commanded Paul to be bound and led off to prison until he should find leisure to give him a more attentive hearing. But Thecla in the night took off her bracelets and gave them to the door-keeper, and when the door was opened for her she went off to the prison. To the gaoler she gave a silver mirror, and so went in to Paul and sat at his feet and heard him proclaim the mighty acts of God .... And the governor was greatly affected. He had Paul scourged.   ACTS OF PAUL 3:2, 5, 7, 16–18, 21

But the people of the city were divided; some sided with the Jews, and some with the apostles. When an attempt was made by both Gentiles and Jews, with their rulers, to molest them and to stone them, they learned of it and fled to Lystra and Derbe, cities of Lycaonia, and to the surrounding country; and there they preached the gospel.

Now at Lystra there was a man sitting, who could not use his feet; he was a cripple from birth, who had never walked. He listened to Paul speaking; and Paul, looking intently at him and seeing that he had faith to be made well, said in a loud voice, "Stand upright on your feet." And he sprang up and walked.

And when the crowds saw what Paul had done, they lifted up their voices, saying in Lycaonian, "The gods have come down to us in the likeness of men!" Barnabas they called Zeus, and Paul, because he was the chief speaker, they called Hermes. And the priest of Zeus, whose temple was in front of the city, brought oxen and garlands to the gates and wanted to offer sacrifice with the people. But when the apostles Barnabas and Paul heard of it, they tore their garments and rushed out among the multitude, crying, "Men, why are you doing this? We also are men, of like nature with you."

But Jews came there from Antioch and Iconium; and having persuaded the people, they stoned Paul and dragged him out of the city, supposing that he was dead. But when the disciples gathered about him, he rose up and entered the city; and on the next day he went on with Barnabas to Derbe.

When they had preached the gospel to that city and had made many disciples, they returned to Lystra and to Iconium and to Antioch, strengthening the souls of the disciples, exhorting them to continue in the faith, and saying that through many tribulations we must enter the kingdom of God. And when they had appointed elders for them in every church, with prayer and fasting they committed them to the Lord in whom they believed.

ACTS 14:4–15, 19–23

Then they passed through Pisidia, and came to Pamphylia. And when they had spoken the word in Perga, they went down to Attalia; and from there they sailed to Antioch, where they had been commended to the grace of God for the work which they had fulfilled.

And when they arrived, they gathered the church together and declared all that God had done with them, and how he had opened a door of faith to the Gentiles. And they remained no little time with the disciples.

ACTS 14:24–28

[Paul reported on his hardships in the second letter to the Corinthians:]

But whatever any one dares to boast of—I am speaking as a fool—I also dare to boast of that. Are they Hebrews? So am I. Are they Israelites? So am I. Are they descendants of Abraham? So am I. Are they servants of Christ? I am a better one—I am talking like a madman—with far greater labors, far more imprisonments, with countless beatings, and often near death. Five times I have received at the hands of the Jews the forty lashes less one. Three times I have been beaten with rods; once I was stoned.

Three times I have been shipwrecked; a night and a day I have been adrift at sea; on frequent journeys, in danger from rivers, danger from robbers, danger from my own people, danger from Gentiles, danger in the city, danger in the wilderness, danger at sea, danger from false brethren; in toil and hardship, through many a sleepless night, in hunger and thirst, often without food, in cold and exposure. And, apart from other things, there is the daily pressure upon me of my anxiety for all the churches. Who is weak, and I am not weak? Who is made to fall, and I am not indignant?

If I must boast, I will boast of the things that show my weakness. The God and Father of the Lord Jesus, he who is blessed for ever, knows that I do not lie.

2 COR 11:21–31

Right: (34) Triple door of the Temple wall in Jerusalem
On the following two pages:
(35) Peter and Paul

The Apostolic Council in Jerusalem

But some men came down from Judea and were teaching the brethren, "Unless you are circumcised according to the custom of Moses, you cannot be saved." And when Paul and Barnabas had no small dissension and debate with them, Paul and Barnabas and some of the others were appointed to go up to Jerusalem to the apostles and the elders about this question.

So, being sent on their way by the church, they passed through both Phoenicia and Samaria, reporting the conversion of the Gentiles, and they gave great joy to all the brethren. When they came to Jerusalem, they were welcomed by the church and the apostles and the elders, and they declared all that God had done with them.   ACTS 15:1–4

But some believers who belonged to the party of the Pharisees rose up, and said, "It is necessary to circumcise them, and to charge them to keep the law of Moses." The apostles and the elders were gathered together to consider this matter. And after there had been much debate, Peter rose and said to them:

"Brethren, you know that in the early days God made choice among you, that by my mouth the Gentiles should hear the word of the gospel and believe. And God who knows the heart bore witness to them, giving them the Holy Spirit just as he did to us; and he made no distinction between us and them, but cleansed their hearts by faith. Now therefore why do you make trial of God by putting a yoke upon the neck of the disciples which neither our fathers nor we have been able to bear? But we believe that we shall be saved through the grace of the Lord Jesus, just as they will."

And all the assembly kept silence; and they listened to Barnabas and Paul as they related what signs and wonders God had done through them among the Gentiles.

ACTS 15:5–12

Left: (36) Christ commissions Peter and Paul

After they finished speaking, James replied, "Brethren, listen to me. Simeon has related how God first visited the Gentiles, to take out of them a people for his name. And with this the words of the prophets agree, as it is written:

'After this I will return, and I will rebuild the dwelling of David, which has fallen; I will rebuild its ruins, and I will set it up, that the rest of men may seek the Lord, and all the Gentiles who are called by my name, says the Lord, who has made these things known from of old.'

"Therefore my judgment is that we should not trouble those of the Gentiles who turn to God, but should write to them to abstain from the pollutions of idols and from unchastity and from what is strangled and from blood. For from early generations Moses has had in every city those who preach him, for he is read every sabbath in the synagogues."

ACTS 15:13–21

Then it seemed good to the apostles and the elders, with the whole church, to choose men from among them and send them to Antioch with Paul and Barnabas. They sent Judas called Barsabbas, and Silas, leading men among the brethren, with the following letter:

"The brethren, both the apostles and the elders, to the brethren who are of the Gentiles in Antioch and Syria and Cilicia, greeting. Since we have heard that some persons from us have troubled you with words, unsettling your minds, although we gave them no instructions, it has seemed good to us, having come to one accord, to choose men and send them to you with our beloved Barnabas and Paul, men who have risked their lives for the sake of our Lord Jesus Christ. We have therefore sent Judas and Silas, who themselves will tell you the same things by word of mouth. For it has seemed good to the Holy Spirit and to us to lay upon you no greater burden than these necessary things: that you abstain from what has been sacrificed to idols and from blood and from what is strangled and from unchastity. If you keep yourselves from these, you will do well. Farewell."

So when they were sent off, they went down to Antioch; and having gathered the congregation together, they delivered the letter. And when they read it, they rejoiced at the exhortation. And Judas and Silas, who were themselves prophets, exhorted the brethren with many words and strengthened them. And after they had spent some time, they were sent off in peace by the brethren to those who had sent them.

But Paul and Barnabas remained in Antioch, teaching and preaching the word of the Lord, with many others also. ACTS 15:22–35

[Paul reported on the meeting in Jerusalem:]

Then after fourteen years I went up again to Jerusalem with Barnabas, taking Titus along with me. I went up by revelation; and I laid before them (but privately before those who were of repute) the gospel which I preach among the Gentiles, lest somehow I should be running or had run in vain. But even Titus, who was with me, was not compelled to be circumcised, though he was a Greek.

And from those who were reputed to be something (what they were makes no difference to me; God shows no partiality)—those, I say, who were of repute added nothing to me; but on the contrary, when they saw that I had been entrusted with the gospel to the uncircumcised, just as Peter had been entrusted with the gospel to the circumcised (for he who worked through Peter for the mission to the circumcised worked through me also for the Gentiles) and when they perceived the grace that was given to me, James and Cephas and John, who were reputed to be pillars, gave to me and Barnabas the right hand of fellowship, that we should go to the Gentiles and they to the circumcised; only they would have us remember the poor, which very thing I was eager to do.

But when Cephas came to Antioch I opposed him to his face, because he stood condemned. For before certain men came from James, he ate with the Gentiles; but when they came he drew back and separated himself, fearing the circumcision party. And with him the rest of the Jews acted insincerely, so that even Barnabas was carried away by their insincerity. But when I saw that they were not straightforward about the truth of the gospel, I said to Cephas before them all, "If you, though a Jew, live like a Gentile and not like a Jew, how can you compel the Gentiles to live like Jews?"   GAL 2:1–3, 6–14

Or is God the God of Jews only? Is he not the God of Gentiles also? Yes, of Gentiles also, since God is one; and he will justify the circumcised on the ground of their faith and the uncircumcised through their faith. Do we then overthrow the law by this faith? By no means! On the contrary, we uphold the law.
                                    ROM 3:29–31

Right: (37) Christians at an agape
On the following two pages:
(38) Mountainous terrain of the Taurus Range
(39) View of Samothrace from Troas

The Second Missionary Journey

And after some days Paul said to Barnabas, "Come, let us return and visit the brethren in every city where we proclaimed the word of the Lord, and see how they are." And Barnabas wanted to take with them John called Mark. But Paul thought best not to take with them one who had withdrawn from them in Pamphylia, and had not gone with them to the work. And there arose a sharp contention, so that they separated from each other; Barnabas took Mark with him and sailed away to Cyprus, but Paul chose Silas and departed, being commended by the brethren to the grace of the Lord.

And he went through Syria and Cilicia, strengthening the churches.

And he came also to Derbe and to Lystra. A disciple was there, named Timothy, the son of a Jewish woman who was a believer; but his father was a Greek. He was well spoken of by the brethren at Lystra and Iconium. Paul wanted Timothy to accompany him; and he took him and circumcised him because of the Jews that were in those places, for they all knew that his father was a Greek.

As they went on their way through the cities, they delivered to them for observance the decisions which had been reached by the apostles and elders who were at Jerusalem.

So the churches were strengthened in the faith, and they increased in numbers daily.

ACTS 15:36–41; 16:1–5

And they went through the region of Phrygia and Galatia, having been forbidden by the Holy Spirit to speak the word in Asia. And when they had come opposite Mysia, they attempted to go into Bithynia, but the Spirit of Jesus did not allow them; so, passing by Mysia, they went down to Troas.

And a vision appeared to Paul in the night: a man of Macedonia was standing beseeching him and saying, "Come over to Macedonia and help us." And when he had seen the vision, immediately we sought to go on into Macedonia, concluding that God had called us to preach the gospel to them.

Setting sail therefore from Troas, we made a direct voyage to Samothrace, and the following day to Neapolis, and from there to Philippi, which is the leading city of the district of Macedonia, and a Roman colony. We remained in this city some days. ACTS 16:6–12

Left: (40) The Bay of Neapolis, where Paul landed in Greece

And on the sabbath day we went outside the gate to the riverside, where we supposed there was a place of prayer; and we sat down and spoke to the women who had come together. One who heard us was a woman named Lydia, from the city of Thyatira, a seller of purple goods, who was a worshiper of God. The Lord opened her heart to give heed to what was said by Paul. And when she was baptized, with her household, she besought us, saying. "If you have judged me to be faithful to the Lord, come to my house and stay."

As we were going to the place of prayer, we were met by a slave girl who had a spirit of divination and brought her owners much gain by soothsaying. She followed Paul and us, crying, "These men are servants of the Most High God, who proclaim to you the way of salvation." And this she did for many days. But Paul was annoyed, and turned and said to the spirit, "I charge you in the name of Jesus Christ to come out of her." And it came out that very hour.

But when her owners saw that their hope of gain was gone, they seized Paul and Silas and dragged them into the market place before the rulers; and when they had brought them to the magistrates they said, "These men are Jews and they are disturbing our city. They advocate customs which it is not lawful for us Romans to accept or practice."

The crowd joined in attacking them; and the magistrates tore the garments off them and gave orders to beat them with rods. And when they had inflicted many blows upon them, they threw them into prison, charging the jailer to keep them safely. Having received this charge, he put them into the inner prison and fastened their feet in the stocks.

But about midnight Paul and Silas were praying and singing hymns to God, and the prisoners were listening to them, and suddenly there was a great earthquake, so that the foundations of the prison were shaken; and immediately all the doors were opened and every one's fetters were unfastened. When the jailer woke and saw that the prison doors were open, he drew his sword and was about to kill himself, supposing that the prisoners had escaped. But Paul cried with a loud voice, "Do not harm yourself, for we are all here."

And he called for lights and rushed in, and trembling with fear he fell down before Paul and Silas, and brought them out and said, "Men, what must I do to be saved?" And they said, "Believe in the Lord Jesus, and you will be saved, you and your household." And they spoke the word of the Lord to him and to all that were in his house. ACTS 16:13–32

Right: (41) The Via Egnatia between Neapolis and Philippi
On the following two pages:
(42) Ruins of the city walls at Philippi   (43) Temple of Athena Nike on the Acropolis of Athens

And he took them the same hour of the night, and washed their wounds, and he was baptized at once, with all his family.

But when it was day, the magistrates sent the police, saying, "Let those men go." And the jailer reported the words to Paul, saying, "The magistrates have sent to let you go; now therefore come out and go in peace." But Paul said to them, "They have beaten us publicly, uncondemned, men who are Roman citizens, and have thrown us into prison; and do they now cast us out secretly? No! let them come themselves and take us out."

The police reported these words to the magistrates, and they were afraid when they heard that they were Roman citizens; so they took them out and asked them to leave the city. So they went out of the prison, and visited Lydia; and when they had seen the brethren, they exhorted them and departed.

Now when they had passed through Amphipolis and Apollonia, they came to Thessalonica, where there was a synagogue of the Jews. And Paul went in, as was his custom, and for three weeks he argued with them from the scriptures, explaining and proving that it was necessary for the Christ to suffer and to rise from the dead, and saying, "This Jesus, whom I proclaim to you, is the Christ." And some of them were persuaded, and joined Paul and Silas; as did a great many of the devout Greeks and not a few of the leading women.

But the Jews were jealous, and taking some wicked fellows of the rabble, they gathered a crowd, set the city in an uproar, and attacked the house of Jason, seeking to bring them out to the people. And when they could not find them, they dragged Jason and some of the brethren before the city authorities, crying, "These men who have turned the world upside down have come here also, and Jason has received them; and they are all acting against the decrees of Caesar, saying that there is another king, Jesus."

And the people and the city authorities were disturbed when they heard this. And when they had taken security from Jason and the rest, they let them go.   ACTS 16:33, 35–40; 17:1–9

Left: (44) Paul

The brethren immediately sent Paul and Silas away by night to Beroea; and when they arrived they went into the Jewish synagogue. Now these Jews were more noble than those in Thessalonica, for they received the word with all eagerness, examining the scriptures daily to see if these things were so. Many of them therefore believed, with not a few Greek women of high standing as well as men.

But when the Jews of Thessalonica learned that the word of God was proclaimed by Paul at Beroea also, they came there too, stirring up and inciting the crowds. Then the brethren immediately sent Paul off on his way to the sea, but Silas and Timothy remained there. Those who conducted Paul brought him as far as Athens; and receiving a command for Silas and Timothy to come to him as soon as possible, they departed.

Now while Paul was waiting for them at Athens, his spirit was provoked within him as he saw that the city was full of idols. So he argued in the synagogue with the Jews and the devout persons, and in the market place every day with those who chanced to be there.

Some also of the Epicurean and Stoic philosophers met him. And some said, "What would this babbler say?" Others said, "He seems to be a preacher of foreign divinities" —because he preached Jesus and the resurrection.

And they took hold of him and brought him to the Areopagus, saying, "May we know what this new teaching is which you present? For you bring some strange things to our ears; we wish to know therefore what these things mean." Now all the Athenians and the foreigners who lived there spent their time in nothing except telling or hearing something new.   ACTS 17:10–21

So Paul, standing in the middle of the Areopagus, said:

"Men of Athens, I perceive that in every way you are very religious. For as I passed along, and observed the objects of your worship, I found also an altar with this inscription, 'To an unknown god.' What therefore you worship as unknown, this I proclaim to you.

"The God who made the world and everything in it, being Lord of heaven and earth, does not live in shrines made by man, nor is he served by human hands, as though he needed anything, since he himself gives to all men life and breath and everything. And he made from one every nation of men to live on all the face of the earth, having, determined allotted periods and the boundaries of their habitation, that they should seek God, in the hope that they might feel after him and find him. Yet he is not far from each one of us, for 'In him we live and move and have our being'; as even some of your poets have said, 'For we are indeed his offspring.'

"Being then God's offspring, we ought not to think that the Deity is like gold, or silver, or stone, a representation by the art and imagination of man.

"The times of ignorance God overlooked, but now he commands all men everywhere to repent, because he has fixed a day on which he will judge the world in righteousness by a man whom he has appointed, and of this he has given assurance to all men by raising him from the dead."

Now when they heard of the resurrection of the dead, some mocked; but others said, "We will hear you again about this."

So Paul went out from among them. But some men joined him and believed, among them Dionysius the Areopagite and a woman named Damaris and others with them.

ACTS 17:22–34

After this he left Athens and and went to Corinth. And he found a Jew named Aquila, a native of Pontus, lately come from Italy with his wife Priscilla, because Claudius had commanded all the Jews to leave Rome. And he went to see them; and because he was of the same trade he stayed with them, and they worked, for by trade they were tentmakers. And he argued in the synagogue every sabbath, and persuaded Jews and Greeks.

When Silas and Timothy arrived from Macedonia, Paul was occupied with preaching, testifying to the Jews that the Christ was Jesus. And when they opposed and reviled him, he shook out his garments and said to them, "Your blood be upon your heads! I am innocent. From now on I will go to the Gentiles."

And he left there and went to the house of a man named Titius Justus, a worshiper of God; his house was next door to the synagogue. Crispus, the ruler of the synagogue, believed in the Lord, together with all his household; and many of the Corinthians hearing Paul believed and were baptized.

And the Lord said to Paul one night in a vision, "Do not be afraid, but speak and do not be silent; for I am with you, and no man shall attack you to harm you; for I have many people in this city."

And he stayed a year and six months, teaching the word of God among them.

ACTS 18:1–11

But when Gallio was proconsul of Achaia, the Jews made a united attack upon Paul and brought him before the tribunal, saying, "This man is persuading men to worship God contrary to the law." But when Paul was about to open his mouth, Gallio said to the Jews, "If it were a matter of wrongdoing or vicious crime, I should have reason to bear with you, O Jews; but since it is a matter of questions about words and names and your own law, see to it yourselves; I refuse to be a judge of these things." And he drove them from the tribunal.

After this Paul stayed many days longer, and then took leave of the brethren and sailed for Syria, and with him Priscilla and Aquila.

ACTS 18:12–16, 18

[In Corinth Paul wrote the first of his letters to his communities:]

Paul, Silvanus, and Timothy, to the church of the Thessalonians in God the Father and the Lord Jesus Christ: Grace to you and peace.

We give thanks to God always for you all, constantly mentioning you in our prayers, remembering before our God and Father your work of faith and labor of love and steadfastness of hope in our Lord Jesus Christ.

For we know, brethren beloved by God, that he has chosen you; for our gospel came to you not only in word, but also in power and in the Holy Spirit and with full conviction. You know what kind of men we proved to be among you for your sake. And you became imitators of us and of the Lord, for you received the word in much affliction, with joy inspired by the Holy Spirit; so that you became an example to all the believers in Macedonia and in Achaja. For not only has the word of the Lord sounded forth from you in Macedonia and Achaia, but your faith in God has gone forth everywhere, so that we need not say anything. For they themselves report concerning us what a welcome we had among you, and how you turned to God from idols, to serve a living and true God, and to wait for his Son from heaven, whom he raised from the dead, Jesus who delivers us from the wrath to come.

For you yourselves know, brethren, that our visit to you was not in vain.

But though we had already suffered and been shamefully treated at Philippi, as you know, we had courage in our God to declare to you the gospel of God in the face of great opposition.

For our appeal does not spring from error or uncleanness, nor is it made with guile; but just as we have been approved by God to be entrusted with the gospel, so we speak, not to please men, but to please God who tests our hearts. For we never used either words of flattery, as you know, or a cloak for greed, as God is witness; nor did we seek glory from men, whether from you or from others, though we might have made demands as apostles of Christ.   1 THES 1:1–10; 2:1–6

And we also thank God constantly for this, that when you received the word of God which you heard from us, you accepted it not as the word of men but as what it really is, the word of God, which is at work in you believers.

Right: (45) Socrates
On the following two pages:
(46) Bema (place of judgment) in Corinth
(47) Site of the ancient city of Colossae

For you, brethren, became imitators of the churches of God in Christ Jesus which are in Judea; for you suffered the same things from your own countrymen as they did from the Jews, who killed both the Lord Jesus and the prophets, and drove us out, and displease God and oppose all men by hindering us from speaking to the Gentiles that they may be saved—so as always to fill up the measure of their sins. But God's wrath has come upon them at last! 1 THES 2:13–16

Finally, brethren, we beseech and exhort you in the Lord Jesus, that as you learned from us how you ought to live and to please God, just as you are doing, you do so more and more. For you know what instructions we gave you through the Lord Jesus.

But concerning love of the brethren you have no need to have any one write to you, for you yourselves have been taught by God to love one another; and indeed you do love all the brethren throughout Macedonia. But we exhort you, brethren, to do so more and more, to aspire to live quietly, to mind your own affairs, and to work with your hands, as we charged you.

But we would not have you ignorant, brethren, concerning those who are asleep, that you may not grieve as others do who have no hope. For since we believe that Jesus died and rose again, even so, through Jesus, God will bring with him those who have fallen asleep. For this we declare to you by the word of the Lord, that we who are alive, who are left until the coming of the Lord, shall not precede those who have fallen asleep. 1 THES 4:1–2, 9–11, 13–15

Now we command you, brethren, in the name of our Lord Jesus Christ, that you keep away from any brother who is living in idleness and not in accord with the tradition that you received from us.

For you yourselves know how you ought to imitate us; we were not idle when we were with you, we did not eat any one's bread without paying, but with toil and labor we worked night and day, that we might not burden any of you. It was not because we have not that right, but to give you in our conduct an example to imitate.

For even when we were with you, we gave you this command: If any one will not work, let him not eat. For we hear that some of you are living in idleness, mere busybodies, not doing any work. Now such persons we command and exhort in the Lord Jesus Christ to do their work in quietness and to earn their own living. 2 THES 3:6–12

Left: (48) Aqueduct near Laodicea

The Third Missionary Journey

When he had landed at Caesarea, he went up and greeted the church, and then went down to Antioch. After spending some time there he departed and went from place to place through the region of Galatia and Phrygia, strengthening all the disciples.

Paul passed through the upper country and came to Ephesus. There he found some disciples. And he said to them, "Did you receive the Holy Spirit when you believed?" And they said, "No, we have never even heard that there is a Holy Spirit." And he said, "Into what then were you baptized?" They said, "Into John's baptism." And Paul said, "John baptized with the baptism of repentance, telling the people to believe in the one who was to come after him, that is, Jesus."

On hearing this, they were baptized in the Name of the Lord Jesus. And when Paul had laid his hands upon them, the Holy Spirit came on them; and they spoke with tongues and prophesied. There were about twelve of them in all.

And he entered the synagogue and for three months spoke boldly, arguing and pleading about the kingdom of God; but when some were stubborn and disbelieved, speaking evil of the Way before the congregation, he withdrew from them, taking the disciples with him, and argued daily in the hall of Tyrannus. This continued for two years, so that all the residents of Asia heard the word of the Lord, both Jews and Greeks.

And God did extraordinary miracles by the hands of Paul, so that handkerchiefs or aprons were carried away from his body to the sick, and diseases left them and the evil spirits came out of them. ACTS 18:22–23; 19:1–11

Right: (49) Artemis of the Ephesians
On the following two pages:
(50) Paul
(51) The theater at Ephesus
(52) Woman of a prominent Ephesian family

Now after these events Paul resolved in the Spirit to pass through Macedonia and Achaia and go to Jerusalem, saying, "After I have been there, I must also see Rome." And having sent into Macedonia two of his helpers, Timothy and Erastus, he himself stayed in Asia for a while.

About that time there arose no little stir concerning the Way. For a man named Demetrius, a silversmith, who made silver shrines of Artemis, brought no little business to the craftsmen. These he gathered together, with the workmen of like occupation, and said, "Men, you know that from this business we have our wealth. And you see and hear that not only at Ephesus but almost throughout all Asia this Paul has persuaded and turned away a considerable company of people, saying that gods made with hands are not gods. And there is danger not only that this trade of ours may come into disrepute but also that the temple of the great goddess Artemis may count for nothing, and that she may even be deposed from her magnificence, she whom all Asia and the world worship."

When they heard this they were enraged, and cried out, "Great is Artemis of the Ephesians!" So the city was filled with the confusion; and they rushed together into the theater, dragging with them Gaius and Aristarchus, Macedonians who were Paul's companions in travel.

Paul wished to go in among the crowd, but the disciples would not let him; some of the Asiarchs also, who were friends of his, sent to him and begged him not to venture into the theater.

Now some cried one thing, some another; for the assembly was in confusion, and most of them did not know why they had come together. Some of the crowd prompted Alexander, whom the Jews had put forward. And Alexander motioned with his hand, wishing to make a defense to the people. But when they recognized that he was a Jew, for about two hours they all with one voice cried out, "Great is Artemis of the Ephesians!"

ACTS 19:21–34

Left: (53) The city walls of Assos; from here Paul sailed to Miletus

And when the town clerk had quieted the crowd, he said, "Men of Ephesus, what man is there who does not know that the city of the Ephesians is temple keeper of the great Artemis, and of the sacred stone that fell from the sky? Seeing then that these things cannot be contradicted, you ought to be quiet and do nothing rash. For you have brought these men here who are neither sacrilegious nor blasphemers of our goddess. If therefore Demetrius and the craftsmen with him have a complaint against any one, the courts are open, and there are proconsuls; let them bring charges against one another. But if you seek anything further, it shall be settled in the regular assembly. For we are in danger of being charged with rioting today, there being no cause that we can give to justify this commotion." And when he had said this, he dismissed the assembly.

After the uproar ceased, Paul sent for the disciples and having exhorted them took leave of them and departed for Macedonia. When he had gone through these parts and had given them much encouragement, he came to Greece. There he spent three months, and when a plot was made against him by the Jews as he was about to set sail for Syria, he determined to return through Macedonia. Sopater of Beroea, the son of Pyrrhus, accompanied him; and of the Thessalonians, Aristarchus and Secundus; and [others]. These went on and were waiting for us at Troas, but we sailed away from Philippi after the days of Unleavened Bread, and in five days we came to them at Troas, where we stayed for seven days.

On the first day of the week, when we were gathered together to break bread, Paul talked with them, intending to depart on the morrow; and he prolonged his speech until midnight.

There were many lights in the upper chamber where we were gathered. And a young man named Eutychus was sitting in the window. He sank into a deep sleep as Paul talked still longer; and being overcome by sleep, he fell down from the third story and was taken up dead. But Paul went down and bent over him, and embracing him said, "Do not be alarmed, for his life is in him." And when Paul had gone up and had broken bread and eaten, he conversed with them a long while, until daybreak, and so departed.

But going ahead to the ship, we set sail for Assos, intending to take Paul aboard there, for so he had arranged, intending himself to go by land. And when he met us at Assos, we took him on board and came to Mitylene. And sailing from there we came the following day opposite Chios; the next day we touched at Samos; and the day after that we came to Miletus. ACTS 19:35–41; 20:1–11, 13–15

And from Miletus he sent to Ephesus and called to him the elders of the church. And when they came to him, he said to them:

"You yourselves know how I lived among you all the time from the first day that I set foot in Asia, serving the Lord with all humility and with tears and with trials which befell me through the plots of the Jews; how I did not shrink from declaring to you anything that was profitable, and teaching you in public and from house to house, testifying both to Jews and to Greeks of repentance to God and of faith in our Lord Jesus Christ.

"And now, behold, I am going to Jerusalem, bound in the Spirit, not knowing what shall befall me there; except that the Holy Spirit testifies to me in every city that imprisonment and afflictions await me. But I do not account my life of any value nor as precious to myself, if only I may accomplish my course and the ministry which I received from the Lord Jesus, to testify to the gospel of the grace of God.

"And now, behold, I know that all you among whom I have gone preaching the kingdom will see my face no more. Therefore I testify to you this day that I am innocent of the blood of all of you, for I did not shrink from declaring to you the whole counsel of God.

"Take heed to yourselves and to all the flock, in which the Holy Spirit has made you overseers, to care for the church of God which he obtained with the blood of his own Son. I know that after my departure fierce wolves will come in among you, not sparing the flock; and from among your own selves will arise men speaking perverse things, to draw away the disciples after them.

"Therefore be alert, remembering that for three years I did not cease night or day to admonish every one with tears. And now I commend you to God and to the word of his grace, which is able to build you up and to give you the inheritance among all those who are sanctified."

And when he had spoken thus, he knelt down and prayed with them all. And they all wept and embraced Paul and kissed him, sorrowing most of all because of the word he had spoken, that they should see his face no more. And they brought him to the ship.

ACTS 20:17–32, 36–38

And when we had parted from them and set sail, we came by a straight course to Cos, and the next day to Rhodes, and from there to Patara. And having found a ship crossing to Phoenicia, we went aboard, and set sail. When we had come in sight of Cyprus, leaving it on the left we sailed to Syria, and landed at Tyre; for there the ship was to unload its cargo. And having sought out the disciples, we stayed there for seven days.

When we had finished the voyage from Tyre, we arrived at Ptolemais; and we greeted the brethren and stayed with them for one day. On the morrow we departed and came to Caesarea; and we entered the house of Philip the evangelist, who was one of the seven, and stayed with him. And he had four unmarried daughters, who prophesied. While we were staying for some days, a prophet named Agabus came down from Judea. And coming to us he took Paul's girdle and bound his own feet and hands, and said, "Thus says the Holy Spirit, 'So shall the Jews at Jerusalem bind the man who owns this girdle and deliver him into the hands of the Gentiles.'" When we heard this, we and the people there begged him not to go up to Jerusalem. Then Paul answered, "What are you doing, weeping and breaking my heart? For I am ready not only to be imprisoned but even to die at Jerusalem for the name of the Lord Jesus."

When we had come to Jerusalem, the brethren received us gladly. On the following day Paul went in with us to James; and all the elders were present. After greeting them, he related one by one the things that God had done among the Gentiles through his ministry.

And when they heard it, they glorified God. And they said to him, "You see, brother, how many thousands there are among the Jews of those who have believed; they are all zealous for the law, and they have been told about you that you teach all the Jews who are among the Gentiles to forsake Moses, telling them not to circumcise their children or observe the customs. What then is to be done? They will certainly hear that you have come.

"Do therefore what we tell you. We have four men who are under a vow; take these men and purify yourself along with them and pay their expenses, so that they may shave their heads. Thus all will know that there is nothing in what they have been told about you but that you yourself live in observance of the law."   ACTS 21:1–4, 7–13, 17–24

Right: (54) Ruins of the ancient harbor of Miletus
On the following two pages:
(55) Bluff on the border between Israel and Lebanon
(56) Tower of the Citadel of Jerusalem

Then Paul took the men, and the next day he purified himself with them and went into the temple, to give notice when the days of purification would be fulfilled and the offering presented for every one of them.

When the seven days were almost completed, the Jews from Asia, who had seen him in the temple, stirred up all the crowd, and laid hands on him, crying out, "Men of Israel, help! This is the man who is teaching men everywhere against the people and the law and this place; moreover he also brought Greeks into the temple, and he has defiled this holy place."

Then all the city was aroused, and the people ran together; they seized Paul and dragged him out of the temple, and at once the gates were shut.

And as they were trying to kill him, word came to the tribune of the cohort that all Jerusalem was in confusion. He at once took soldiers and centurions, and ran down to them; and when they saw the tribune and the soldiers, they stopped beating Paul. Then the tribune came up and arrested him, and ordered him to be bound with two chains. He inquired who he was and what he had done. Some in the crowd shouted one thing, some another; and as he could not learn the facts because of the uproar, he ordered him to be brought into the barracks. And when he came to the steps, he was actually carried by the soldiers because of the violence of the crowd; for the mob of the people followed, crying, "Away with him!"

As Paul was about to be brought into the barracks, he said to the tribune, "May I say something to you?" And he said, "Do you know Greek? Are you not the Egyptian, then, who recently stirred up a revolt and led the four thousand men of the Assassins out into the wilderness?" Paul replied, "I am a Jew, from Tarsus in Cilicia, a citizen of no mean city; I beg you, let me speak to the people."

ACTS 21:26–28, 30–39

And when he had given him leave, Paul, standing on the steps, motioned with his hand to the people; and when there was a great hush, he spoke to them in the Hebrew language, saying:

"Brethren and fathers, hear the defense which I now make before you." And when they heard that he addressed them in the Hebrew language, they were the more quiet. And he said: "I am a Jew, born at Tarsus in Cilicia, but brought up in this city at the feet of Gamaliel, educated according to the strict manner of the law of our fathers, being zealous for God as you all are this day."

ACTS 21:40; 22:1–3

Left: (57) Paul
(58) Stairs on the Temple grounds in Jerusalem

[Paul reported on his conversion and then continued:]

"When I had returned to Jerusalem and was praying in the temple, I fell into a trance and saw him saying to me, 'Make haste and get quickly out of Jerusalem, because they will not accept your testimony about me.' And I said, 'Lord, they themselves know that in every synagogue I imprisoned and beat those who believed in thee. And when the blood of Stephen thy witness was shed, I also was standing by and approving, and keeping the garments of those who killed him.' And he said to me, 'Depart; for I will send you far away to the Gentiles.'"

Up to this word they listened to him; then they lifted up their voices and said, "Away with such a fellow from the earth! For he ought not to live."

And as they cried out and waved their garments and threw dust into the air, the tribune commanded him to be brought into the barracks, and ordered him to be examined by scourging, to find out why they shouted thus against him. But when they had tied him up with the thongs, Paul said to the centurion who was standing by, "Is it lawful for you to scourge a man who is a Roman citizen, and uncondemned?"

When the centurion heard that, he went to the tribune and said to him, "What are you about to do? For this man is a Roman citizen." So the tribune came and said to him, "Tell me, are you a Roman citizen?" And he said, "Yes." The tribune answered, "I bought this citizenship for a large sum." Paul said, "But I was born a citizen."

So those who were about to examine him withdrew from him instantly; and the tribune also was afraid, for he realized that Paul was a Roman citizen and that he had bound him.

ACTS 22:17–29

Right: (59) Paul under arrest

116

But on the morrow, desiring to know the real reason why the Jews accused him, he unbound him, and commanded the chief priests and all the council to meet, and he brought Paul down and set him before them.

And Paul, looking intently at the council, said, "Brethren, I have lived before God in all good conscience up to this day." And the high priest Ananias commanded those who stood by him to strike him on the mouth. Then Paul said to him, "God shall strike you, you whitewashed wall! Are you sitting to judge me according to the law, and yet contrary to the law you order me to be struck?"

But when Paul perceived that one part were Sadducees and the other Pharisees, he cried out in the council, "Brethren, I am a Pharisee, a son of Pharisees; with respect to the hope and the resurrection of the dead I am on trial." And when he had said this, a dissension arose, between the Pharisees and the Sadducees; and the assembly was divided. For the Sadducees say that there is no resurrection, nor angel, nor spirit; but the Pharisees acknowledge them all. Then a great clamor arose; and some of the scribes of the Pharisees' party stood up and contended, "We find nothing wrong in this man. What if a spirit or an angel spoke to him?"

And when the dissension became violent, the tribune, afraid that Paul would be torn in pieces by them, commanded the soldiers to go down and take him by force from among them and bring him into the barracks.

The following night the Lord stood by him and said, "Take courage, for as you have testified about me at Jerusalem, so you must bear witness also at Rome."

Left: (60) The ancient harbor of Caesarea

When it was day, the Jews made a plot and bound themselves by an oath neither to eat nor drink till they had killed Paul.

Then he called two of the centurions and said, "At the third hour of the night get ready two hundred soldiers with seventy horsemen and two hundred spearmen to go as far as Caesarea."

So the soldiers, according to their instructions, took Paul and brought him by night to Antipatris. And on the morrow they returned to the barracks, leaving the horsemen to go on with him. When they came to Caesarea and delivered the letter to the governor, they presented Paul also before him. On reading the letter, he asked to what province he belonged. When he learned that he was from Cilicia he said, "I will hear you when your accusers arrive." And he commanded him to be guarded in Herod's praetorium.

ACTS 22:30; 23:1–3, 6–12, 23, 31–35

And after five days the high priest Ananias came down with some elders and a spokesman, one Tertullus. They laid before the governor their case against Paul.... And when the governor had motioned him to speak, Paul replied:

"Realizing that for many years you have been judge over this nation, I cheerfully make my defense. As you may ascertain, it is not more than twelve days since I went up to worship at Jerusalem; and they did not find me disputing with any one or stirring up a crowd, either in the temple or in the synagogues, or in the city. Neither can they prove to you what they now bring up against me.

"But this I admit to you, that according to the Way, which they call a sect, I worship the God of our fathers, believing everything laid down by the law or written in the prophets, having a hope in God which these themselves accept, that there will be a resurrection of both the just and the unjust."

But Felix, having a rather accurate knowledge of the Way, put them off.

But when two years had elapsed, Felix was succeeded by Porcius Festus.... But Festus, wishing to do the Jews a favor, said to Paul, "Do you wish to go up to Jerusalem, and there be tried on these charges before me?"

But Paul said, "I am standing before Caesar's tribunal, where I ought to be tried; to the Jews I have done no wrong, as you know very well. If then I am a wrongdoer, and have committed anything for which I deserve to die, I do not seek to escape death; but if there is nothing in their charges against me, no one can give me up to them. I appeal to Caesar."

Then Festus, when he had conferred with his council, answered, "You have appealed to Caesar; to Caesar you shall go."

ACTS 24:1, 10–15, 22, 27; 25:9–12

And when it was decided that we should sail for Italy, they delivered Paul and some other prisoners to a centurion of the Augustan Cohort, named Julius. And embarking in a ship of Adramyttium, which was about to sail to the ports along the coast of Asia, we put to sea.

Right: (61) Ship leaving a harbor

The Journey to Rome

As much time had been lost, and the voyage was already dangerous because the fast had already gone by, Paul advised them, saying, "Sirs, I perceive that the voyage will be with injury and much loss, not only of the cargo and the ship, but also of our lives." But the centurion paid more attention to the captain and to the owner of the ship than to what Paul said.

And when the south wind blew gently, supposing that they had obtained their purpose, they weighed anchor and sailed along Crete, close inshore. But soon a tempestuous wind, called the northeaster, struck down from the land.... And when neither sun nor stars appeared for many a day, and no small tempest lay on us, all hope of our being saved was at last abandoned.

As they had been long without food, Paul then came forward among them and said, "Men, you should have listened to me, and should not have set sail from Crete and incurred this injury and loss. I now bid you take heart; for there will be no loss of life among you, but only of the ship. For this very night there stood by me an angel of the God to whom I belong and whom I worship, and he said, 'Do not be afraid, Paul; you must stand before Caesar; and lo, God has granted you all those who sail with you.' So take heart, men, for I have faith in God that it will be exactly as I have been told."

Left: (62) Paul with the viper on Malta

Now when it was day, they did not recognize the land, but they noticed a bay with a beach, on which they planned if possible to bring the ship ashore.... But striking a shoal they ran the vessel aground; the bow stuck and remained immovable, and the stern was broken up by the surf.

After we had escaped, we then learned that the island was called Malta. And the natives showed us unusual kindness, for they kindled a fire and welcomed us all, because it had begun to rain and was cold. Paul had gathered a bundle of sticks and put them on the fire, when a viper came out because of the heat and fastened on his hand.

When the natives saw the creature hanging from his hand, they said to one another, "No doubt this man is a murderer. Though he has escaped from the sea, justice has not allowed him to live."

He, however, shook off the creature into the fire and suffered no harm. They waited, expecting him to swell up or suddenly fall down dead; but when they had waited a long time and saw no misfortune come to him, they changed their minds and said that he was a god.

ACTS 27:1–2, 9–11, 13–14, 21–25, 39, 41; 28:1–6

After three months we set sail in a ship which had wintered in the island, a ship of Alexandria, with the Twin Brothers as figurehead. Putting in at Syracuse, we stayed there for three days. And from there we made a circuit and arrived at Rhegium; and after one day a south wind sprang up, and on the second day we came to Puteoli. There we found brethren, and were invited to stay with them for seven days. And so we came to Rome.

And the brethren there, when they heard of us, came as far as the Forum of Appius and Three Taverns to meet us. On seeing them Paul thanked God and took courage. And when we came into Rome, Paul was allowed to stay by himself, with the soldier that guarded him.   ACTS 28:11–16

There were awaiting Paul at Rome Luke from Gaul and Titus from Dalmatia. When Paul saw them he was glad, so that he hired a barn outside Rome, where with the brethren he taught the word of truth. The news was spread abroad, and many souls were added to the Lord.

But a certain Patroclus, Caesar's cup-bearer, came late to the barn and, being unable because of the crowd to go in to Paul, sat at a high window and listened to him teaching the word of God. But since the wicked devil was envious of the love of the brethren, Patroclus fell from the window and died, and the news was quickly brought to Nero.

Paul said to them [the crowd]: "Now, brethren, let your faith be manifest. Come, all of you, let us mourn to our Lord Jesus Christ, that this youth may live and we remain unmolested." But as they all lamented the youth drew breath again, and setting him upon a beast they sent him back alive with the others who were of Caesar's house.... And when Caesar heard that Patroclus was alive he was afraid, and did not want to go in. But when he had entered he saw Patroclus and, beside himself, cried out: "Patroclus, art thou alive?" And he said: "I am alive, Caesar." But he said: "Who is he who made thee to live?" And the youth, borne by the conviction of faith, said: "Christ Jesus, the king of the ages."

Right: (63) The Italian coast near Pozzuoli
On the following four pages:
(64) The Via Appia near Rome
(65) The Temple of Vesta in the Forum at Rome
(66) Peter and Paul before Nero

The Martyrdom of Paul

But he [Nero] shut them [Patroclus and three of Nero's chief men] up in prison, after torturing dreadfully men whom he greatly loved, and commanded that the soldiers of the great king be sought out, and he issued a decree to this effect, that all who were found to be Christians and soldiers of Christ should be put to death.

And among the many Paul also was brought bound; to him all his fellow-prisoners gave heed, so that Caesar observed that he was the man in command. And he said to him: "Man of the great king, but (now) my prisoner, why did it seem good to thee to come secretly into the empire of the Romans and enlist soldiers from my province?" But Paul, filled with the Holy Spirit, said before them all: "Caesar, not only from thy province do we enlist soldiers, but from the whole world. For this charge has been laid upon us, that no man be excluded who wishes to serve my king. If thou also think it good, do him service! for neither riches nor the splendour of this present life will save thee, but if thou submit and entreat him, then shalt thou be saved. For in one day he will destroy the world with fire."

When Caesar heard this, he commanded all the prisoners to be burned with fire, but Paul to be beheaded according to the law of the Romans.

Then Paul stood with his face to the east, and lifting up his hands to heaven prayed at length; and after communing in prayer in Hebrew with the fathers he stretched out his neck without speaking further. But when the executioner struck off his head, milk spurted upon the soldier's clothing. And when they saw it, the soldier and all who stood by were amazed, and glorified God who had given Paul such glory. And they went off and reported to Caesar what had happened.

ACTS OF PAUL 11:1–3, 5

On the preceding two pages:
(67) Paul is led to execution
(68) The Roman she-wolf
Left: (69) Saint Paul the Apostle

INDEX
OF
ILLUSTRATIONS

8 Stairway of the Temple of Augustus in Samaria-Sebaste. The temple, built by Herod the Great, possessed an unwalled forecourt seventy meters square. Beyond the forecourt lay a free-standing stairway 25 meters in width. By ascending its 24 steps the visitor gained access to the temple proper.

13 The wilderness of Judea in the region of the Wadi El-Kelt. The remains of a Roman aqueduct are seen.

9 A bust of Paul, worked in relief on a bronze plaque dating from the 7th century. The Apostle is portrayed with nimbus and is clad in tunic and cloak. In his left hand he holds a book; the right hand is laid across his breast. The inscription reads Ο ΠΑΥΛΟΣ. Bronze: length: 4.1 cm. London, British Museum.

10 The Damascus Road, between Gamala and El-Kuneitra in Syria. This road was traveled by Paul.

11 The conversion of Paul, depicted on a medieval casket cover. There are seven surviving sections (cf. nos. 12, 25, 66) of a series of enameled plaques portraying scenes from the lives and legends of Peter and Paul. The plaques are of English provenance, dating from ca. 1180–85. They originally adorned a reliquary or altar. Champlevé enamel: length: 12.7 cm.; width: 8.6 cm. Lyon, Musée des Beaux-Arts, Cat. 1887–188.

14 Busts of Peter and Paul on an unfinished 4th-century limestone relief. The Apostles (Peter on the left, Paul on the right) are shown in profile, facing one another. Limestone: length: 57 cm.; depth: 14 cm. Aquilea, Museo Archeologico. Photograph from a copy in the Museo della Civiltà Romana, Rome.

12 Paul's flight in a basket from imprisonment in Damascus (cf. no. 11). London, Victoria and Albert Museum, M. 312–1926.

15 Tarsus, the birthplace of Paul. Tradition holds that it was founded by Greeks in the Archaic Period. After 1200 B.C., it became an important Hittite city. While under Seleucid rule, it became a center of Stoic philosophy. After 65 B.C., under Roman dominion, it was the capital of Cilicia. The photograph shows the remains of the Roman city gate.

16 Antioch on the Orontes was founded in 300 B.C. by King Seleukos I. For a time it was the capital of the Seleucid Empire which comprised a portion of the conquests of Alexander the Great. The city had a large Jewish colony and became an early center. From here Paul and Barnabas embarked on their missionary journeys. The modern city of Antakya completely covers the structures of the Roman and early Christian period. The photograph shows the Orontes near Antioch.

17 Section of a Roman sarcophagus of the 2nd–3rd century A.D. A ship is shown sailing against the waves, while three sailors are busy steering and trimming the sales. Dolphins, a dinghy, and a man who has fallen overboard are seen between the waves. Marble: height: 52 cm.; length: 178 cm.; depth: 54 cm. Copenhagen, Ny-Carlsberg-Glyptothek, Inv. 1299. Photograph from a copy in Rome, Museo della Civiltà Romana.

18 Columns of the Roman forum in Salamis (near Famagusta) on Cyprus. Paul and Barnabas landed here at the beginning of their first missionary journey. Cyprus was the home of Barnabas and was probably also the site of his martyrdom after his parting with Paul.

19 Peter and Paul on a gilded glass fragment from the late 4th century. The two apostles, clean-shaven and short-haired, are shown seated opposite one another within an octagonal frame. The legend reads PAUSUS and CRITSUS, identifying Peter as the representative of Christ. Whitish glass with gilding: 9.3 cm. × 5.3 cm. Bologna, Museo Civico.

20 Roman Governor, in a scene depicting a census in Bethlehem. Section of a mosaic lunette in the exonarthex (ante-chamber for the unbaptized) of the Church of St. Savior in the Chora (Kahrie Djami) in Istanbul. The mosaics and frescoes of the Church of St. Savior were created ca. 1315–1320 by an endowment from Theodoros Metochites. They represent the most significant monument of Palaeologan art. The arches and wall of the church are covered with scenes depicting the life of Mary and the youth and miracles of Christ. In the 15th century the church was turned into a mosque. It is now a museum. Istanbul, Kahrie Djami.

21 Atallia (Antalya), founded in the 2nd century B.C. by Attalus II of Pergamum, was an important port in ancient times. Paul, coming from Cyprus, landed here to inaugurate his first missionary journey in Asia Minor. The photograph shows the bay of Atallia with the Lycian Taurus Range in the background.

22 Perga, one of the most important archaeological sites in Pamphylia. According to legend, Perga was founded by the Greeks after the Trojan War, but it became an important city only after the time of Alexander the Great. From 188 B.C. onwards it was part of the Roman Empire. Paul visited Perga several times in the course of his missionary journeys. The photograph shows the ruins of a gate tower built in the Hellenistic period.

23 Pisidian Antioch was founded shortly before 280 B.C. by Seleukos Nikator, probably on the site of an ancient Phrygian sanctuary. The city became part of the Roman Empire in about 27 B.C. and flourished under the patronage of Augustus. The ancient city was destroyed in A.D.713 in the course of the Arab invasions. Archaeological excavations have been conducted by the University of Michigan. The photograph shows the remains of the Roman aqueduct (1st century A.D.). Paul visited the city a number of times on his missionary journeys.

24 Ruins of the Jewish synagogue (3rd century) at Qazrin in the Golan region. The synagogues of Pisidian Antioch and other sites of the Pauline mission may have possessed similar architectural features.

25 Paul in disputation with Greeks and Jews (cf. no. 11). London, Victoria and Albert Museum, M. 233–1874.

26 Paul under threat. Section of an arcaded sarcophagus depicting the martyrdoms of Peter and Paul, with Christ as teacher in the central scene. The sarcophagus, dating from the 4th century, now contains the relics of a companion of St. Maurice. Carrera marble: length: 210 cm.; height: 60 cm.; depth: 65 cm. Marseilles, Crypt of St. Victor.

27 Iconium (Konya), where Paul met Thecla. Iconium is one of the most ancient cities of Asia Minor, with a history of settlement dating back to the third millennium B.C. The city has had an eventful history. It was an episcopal see in the Byzantine period and later the capital of a Sultanate. Crusaders occupied it under Frederick Barbarossa, and the order of dancing dervishes originated there. The modern city has a population of over 200,000. The illustration shows a view of the citadel of Iconium.

28 Paul is shown seated on a stone before a city gate. Thecla is leaning over the gate in order to listen to him. Section of a side panel of an ivory casket dating from ca. A.D. 420–430. The casket depicts Moses striking water from the rock together with scenes from the lives of Peter and Paul (cf. no. 31) Ivory: height: 4.2 cm.; width: 9.8 cm. London, British Museum.

29 A scene of sacrifice on a work of bronze appliqué dating from the 2nd century A.D. A bull adorned for sacrifice is seen between the priest and the sacrificial attendant. Bronze: height: 14.5 cm.; width: 13.5 cm.; depth: 2 cm.; Szombathely, Savaria-Museum, Inv. 54,627.

30 Paul, from a scene which portrays Christ enthroned between Peter and Paul. Fresco (late 4th century) in the Catacomb of Peter and Marcellinus, Rome.

31 Stoning of Paul. Section of the side panel of an ivory casket (cf. no. 28). The view of this scene is separated from the Thecla scene by a curve in the side of the casket.

32 View of the Lycian Taurus Range from Perga (cf. no. 38).

35 Representations of the Apostles Peter and Paul incised on the tombstone of a six-year-old boy named Asellus (4th century). The Chrismon appears between the two bearded figures (Peter at the left, Paul at the right). Rome, Lateran. Photograph from a copy in Rome, Museo della Civiltà Romana.

33 Detail from a medieval portable altar. Paul is shown seated beneath a low, richly ornamented arch. The altar is an oak chest covered with gilded plates of thin silver. Each of the long sides of the altar bears engraved representations of five apostles, with Peter and Paul at the center. The names of the apostles are rendered in niello along the border of the plate which covers the lid. The portable altar, dating from 1100, was the work of Roger von Helmarshausen. Height: 16.5 cm.; length: 34.5 cm.; width: 21.2 cm. Paderborn, Domschatz.

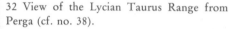

36 Section of the sarcophagus of Junius Bassus, Prefect of Rome (died A. D. 359). The Bassus sarcophagus is the most important example of the two-tiered, arcaded sarcophagus; its draped and nude figures are rendered in very high relief in an organic, three-dimensional treatment of the subjects. The middle scene of the upper tier portrays the regnant Christ entrusting the laws to Peter and Paul (cf. no. 67). Pentelic marble: length: 243 cm.; height: 141 cm. Vatican City, Grotto of St. Peter.

34 The triple door on the south side of the Temple grounds in Jerusalem.

37 A Christian love-feast. Fresco (second half of the 2nd century) in the Catacomb of Callistus, Rome.

38 The mountainous terrain of the Taurus Range, crossed repeatedly by Paul in the course of his journeys. The Taurus Range rises in the southern highlands of Asia Minor, then drops off (sharply at some points) along the Mediterranean coast. It reaches heights of 3,200 m. in the Lycian Taurus (Bey Dagh) and 3,585 m. in the Cilician Taurus (Bulgar Dagh).

39 View of the Hellenistic-Roman ruins of Troas, 40 km. southeast of ancient Troy. Paul set out from here on his journey via Samothrace to Macedonia (Acts 16:11).

40 The Bay of Neapolis. It was here, in the course of his second missionary journey, that Paul first set foot on Graeco-European soil. Neapolis is now known as Kavalla and has a population of approximately 60,000. The city served as a naval base in Roman times, but there are no significant remains dating from that period.

41 The Via Egnatia near Neapolis. This Roman road was a continuation of the Italian Via Appia. It was the most important route from the west coast of Greece, passing through Macedonia to link Dyrrhachium with Byzantium.

42 Ruins of the ancient city walls at Philippi. The ancient city, originally named Krenides, was founded by Thasos. In 356 B.C. it was renamed Philippi in honor of King Philip II of Macedonia. In the Roman period, when Paul visited the city, Philippi was an important military colony. The city went into decline in the Middle Ages.

43 The Temple of Athena Nike (ca. 430 B.C.) on the Acropolis of Athens.

44 Paul. Detail of a portable altar from the Abdinghof Cloister. The altar, an oak chest with engraved and excised copper gilt plates, is the work of Roger von Helmarshausen, ca. 1100. Two separate niches, one set over the other, appear on either side of the altar. On one side, Paul is shown above Felix, on the other Peter above St. Blaise (patron of the Abdinghof Cloister). Height: 11.8 cm.; length: 13 cm.; width: 18.5 cm. Paderborn, Franciscan Church.

45 Wall painting from a house in Ephesus. The Greek philosopher Socrates, clad in a white mantle, is shown seated on a marble bench. The name Socrates appears above the figure. The Roman fresco (A.D. 60–80) bears evidence of later graffiti, among them a Christian inscription. Fresco: height (of figure): 34 cm. Selçuk, Archaeological Museum, Inv. 1574.

46 The Bema, the place where the Roman governor held court, in the agora at Corinth. Here the governor Gallio heard and dismissed the Jewish accusation against Paul (Acts 18:12ff.). The history of Corinth may be traced back to the Stone Age. In 146 B.C. the city became a Roman possession and served as seat of the proconsul of Achaia. The city came into even greater prominence under the Emperor Hadrian. Due to Paul's presence, Corinth became an important center of early Christianity. The illustration shows a view of the Bema amidst the ruins of the Graeco-Roman agora on the Acro-Corinth.

47 Colossae was founded by the successors of Alexander the Great. After the city suffered severe devastation in an earthquake in A.D. 60, its inhabitants rebuilt on the slope of the Honaz Daği. Colossae was probably Christianized from Ephesus. In the epistle to the Colossians, Paul, who had not visited the city, spoke out against a heresy which had taken root there. The illustration shows the Honaz plateau, site of the ancient city.

48 Laodicea was founded in the 3rd century B.C. Archaeologists from the University of Quebec have uncovered numerous remains from the Roman period. At the time, the city had a large Jewish colony, which probably accounts for the rapid Christianization which took place under Paul's disciple Epaphras. Paul greets the city, which is numbered among the "seven churches of Asia" (Rev. 3:14) in the epistle to the Colossians. The illustration shows the Roman aqueduct near Laodicea.

49 The larger than life-size statue of Artemis of the Ephesians (the so-called "Great Artemis") is a copy of the wooden cult image which stood in the Artemision in Roman times (mid-2nd century A.D.). In order to prevent the statue from falling into Christian hands, the devotees of the goddess gave the image a cultic burial in the Prytaneion, the seat of supreme religious authority in Ephesus. Marble: Height: 292 cm. Selçuk, Archaeological Museum, Inv. 712.

50 Paul on an ivory tablet dating from the 6th century. Beneath an arcade with shell motif is a *tabula ansata* bearing the inscription SCS PAULUS (St. Paul); this rests on two chamfered columns. The Apostle, wearing a long tunic, mantle, and sandals, stands before a drape, his right hand raised in blessing, his left holding a book adorned with a cross. Ivory: height: 32.8 cm.; width: 13.4 cm. Paris, Musée de Cluny.

51 The theater, center of cultural life, at Ephesus. The theater was the focal point of the disturbance incited by Demetrius the silversmith against Paul and his adherents (Acts 19:23ff.). The original Hellenistic structure was substantially rebuilt and enlarged in the Roman period (1st and 2nd centuries A.D.). The view is to the south, toward the amphitheater, orchestra, and scene-front, with the Bülbüldağ in the background.

52 The female portrait statue from the period of Trajan (first half of the 2nd century A.D.) is part of the statuary adorning a fountain complex in Ephesus, the Nymphaeum Traiani. The statue probably represents a member of the family which endowed the building. The female figure, dressed in a long undergarment (chiton) and mantle, was worked in stock and provided with the appropriate portrait head as needed. Marble: height: 204 cm. Selçuk, Archaeological Museum, Inv. 1404.

53 Assos was established as a colony in the Archaic Period by Greeks from the adjacent island of Mytilene (Lesbos). It never played an important role in history. On return from Macedonia, after a stop in Troas, Paul met here with his comrades who had traveled by ship. They sailed on together to Miletus. The illustration shows the formidable city walls which date from the 4th century B.C.

54 Miletus was one of the most ancient and important Greek cities on the coast of Asia Minor. It was perhaps originally settled by Mycenaeans from Crete. The city, which itself established various colonies on the Black Sea, played an important role in the Persian War. After its destruction in 494 B.C., Miletus was rebuilt in the pattern of a rectangular grid according to plans drawn up by Hippodamus of Miletus. In 334 B.C. the city, which was also famous for its philosophical school (Thales, Anaximander, Anaximenes), was conquered by Alexander the Great. It came under Roman rule in 190. The city declined after the 10th century. Its ancient remains were excavated in 1899 by T. Wiegand. The illustration shows ruins of the ancient harbor on the shore of the Maeander River.

55 The white rocks of Rosh Hanikra, a bluff on the present border between Israel and Lebanon. In Paul's time, as now, they were an important landmark for coastal navigation.

56 The Phasael Tower of the so-called Citadel of Jerusalem. The fortress, built in the 14th century and enlarged by Suleiman the Magnificent in 1532, stands on the foundations of the palace erected by Herod the Great in 24 B.C. The tower is named after Herod's brother Phasael. The Mariamne and Hippieus towers, named after the king's wife and an intimate friend, are also preserved to the present day.

57 Paul, from a scene which shows Sixtus II between Peter and Paul. Fresco (ca. 348) in the Catacomb of Domitilla, Rome.

58 Stairs to the bridge on the west side of the Temple (Robinson Bridge), connecting the Temple Mount with the upper city.

59 The arrest of Paul. A Roman soldier places a rope around the Apostle's neck. Section from a resurrection sarcophagus with scenes from the martyrdoms of Peter and Paul. The sarcophagus dates from the late 4th century. It now contains the relics of the martyrs Chrysanthus and Darius. Carrera marble: length: 213 cm.; height: 58 cm. Marseilles, Crypt of St. Victor.

60 Caesarea was an important port in Phoenician times. It maintained this role also in the Seleucid period. In 22–10 B.C. it was enlarged by Herod the Great, becoming an imposing city and port facility. The illustration shows the Straton Tower (the city was so named prior to Herod) and remains of the ancient port complex.

61 Mosaic showing a ship in harbor. In the foreground is a long mole with arches, to the left a lighthouse with a statue at the top. To the right of the tower is seen the stern of a ship, a bireme (perhaps a votive ship) leaving the harbor. The sails are set, the sailors are inspecting the rigging, and the helmsman is standing at the rudder. The large mosaic, made of marble and enameled stones, adorned the *nymphaeum* of the house of T. Claudius Claudianus on the Quirinal. The mosaic dates from ca. A.D. 200 Length: 212 cm.; width: 190 cm. Rome, Palazzo dei Conservatori, upper gallery.

62 Paul with the viper (cf. Acts 28:3 ff.). Fresco (10th century) in the Chapel of St. Anselm, Canterbury Cathedral.

63 View of the Italian coast near Pozzuoli (Puteoli), near Naples. In Roman times there was an important harbor here, where Paul landed on his journey to Rome. Paul found that there was already a Christian community at Puteoli.

66 The Apostles Peter and Paul before Nero (cf. no. 11). Dijon, Musée des Beaux-Arts, Collection Trimolet, no. 1250.

67 Paul is led away. The reeds in the background suggest the marshes of the Tiber as the traditional place of execution. Scene from the lower tier of the Junius Bassus sarcophagus (cf. no. 36).

64 The Via Appia is the most famous of the great Roman roads. Its name derives from the Censor Appius Claudius, who began its construction in 312 B.C. The road leads from Rome via Capua, Benevent, to Brindisi. It was completed in 191 B.C. Near Rome the road is flanked by many tombs and by the entrances to various Christian catacombs.

68 The Roman she-wolf who suckled the twins Romulus and Remus (original in the Capitoline Museum, Rome). The bronze figure was probably cast by Etruscan metalsmiths ca. 470 B.C. (the twins were added ca. 1500, perhaps by A. Pollaiuolo). Many copies have been found throughout the sphere of Roman domination, for the figure was understood as a symbol of the Roman Empire. Paul's great achievement consisted in bringing Christianity to this world empire.

65 The Temple of Vesta in the Forum Romanum at Rome.

69 Paul on the side of a reliquary made in the shape of a house. The reliquary is of Catalonian workmanship, dating from the first quarter of the 12th century. The Apostle (SAĊTVS PAVLVS APOSTOLVS) stands in a frontal pose, right hand uplifted, left hand holding a book. Copper plate with champlevé enamel and gilding: height 22.5 cm.; width: 11.3 cm. Dijon, Musée des Beaux-Arts, Collection Trimolet, no. 1878.